FAVOURITE ANNUAL FLOWERS

Golden Hands Books

Marshall Cavendish
London and New York

Picture credits
A–Z Tourist Photo Library: pages 11, 57, 68
D. C. Arminson: pages 51, 53, 54, 57, 61, 62,
    63, 66, 71, 72, 73, 74, 77, 88, 89
Barnaby's Picture Library: pages 27, 34
Carlo Bevilacqua: pages 56, 60, 86
Antony Birks: page 63
Blackmore & Langdon: page 41
D. V. Blogg: page 61
P. Booth: page 64
R. J. Corbin: pages 8, 9, 10, 51, 52, 61, 72, 88,
    89
J. K. D. Cowley: page 86
A. F. Derrick: page 51
Gordon Douglas: pages 43, 48, 81
J. E. Downward: pages 18, 41, 50, 59, 62, 79,
    80, 82, 84
Valerie Finnis: pages 16, 17, 23, 24, 49, 55, 65,
    77, 82, 85, 94
Paul Genereux: pages 45, 47
A. P. Hamilton: page 54
Iris Hardwick: page 42
H. R. Hood: page 40
Peter Hunt: pages 7, 12, 15, 19, 34, 36, 51, 66,
    97, 98
A. J. Huxley: pages 51, 71, 75, 79, 81
George E. Hyde: pages 26, 33, 44, 59, 66, 69
Leslie Johns: pages 19, 33, 39
Reginald Kaye: page 72
N. Kelly: page 66
D. J. Kesby: pages 76, 85
Ministry of Agriculture: page 11
H. Alan Morrison: page 70
Frank Naylor: page 87
Opera Mundi: page 40
Ronald Parrett: pages 55, 96
Picturepoint: page 22
Christopher Reynolds: pages 50, 69
Ruth Rutter: page 76
D. Smith: page 50
Harry Smith: pages 7, 10, 12, 13, 14, 15, 16, 17,
    20, 21, 23, 24, 25, 26, 29, 30, 31, 32, 35, 37,
    38, 40, 42, 44, 46, 48, 49, 54, 55, 56, 58, 60,
    65, 67, 68, 70, 77, 78, 83, 84, 86, 87, 88, 89,
    92, 93, 98
Violet Stevenson: page 68
D. Wildridge: page 91
C. Williams: page 67
Dennis Woodland: pages 64, 70, 72

Edited by Maggi McCormick

Published by
Marshall Cavendish Publications Limited,
58 Old Compton Street, London W1V 5PA

© Marshall Cavendish Limited 1968–69–70–73
This material was first published
by Marshall Cavendish Limited
in *Encyclopedia of Gardening*

This volume first published 1975

**Printed in Great Britain by
Ben Johnson & Company Ltd., York.**

ISBN 0 85685 096 9

Salvia splendons

Introduction

Quick-growing, colourful, long-lasting — annual flowers are a beautiful way to brighten up any garden. Because they are replaced each year, annuals provide lots of versatility, and they are a fast and inexpensive way to give colour and vibrancy to a new garden while slower-growing herbaceous flowers and shrubs establish themselves.

Favourite Annual Flowers is a gardener's handbook, an alphabetical listing of more than 100 popular annuals and specific hints for successful cultivation of each one. There are chapters on using annuals as cut flowers, on growing 'Everlasting' annuals to dry and an indispensable section of general information.

Contents

Chapter	Page
Annuals	7
Planting	8
Cloches	10
Fragrant annuals	11
Bedding out	11
Borders	12
Biennials	13
The Flowers from Ageratum to Zinnia	15
Everlasting flowers	92
Cut flowers	96

Godetia 'Dwarf Double Mixture'

Eschscholtzia 'Double Hybrid'

ANNUALS

Hardy annuals are easy to grow and will give a quick and brilliant display provided they are grown in an open, sunny position in any good garden soil. Many annuals are tender and easily killed by frost, so these kinds are sown under glass in the spring and planted out when all danger of frost is over. Some hardy and half-hardy kinds make excellent pot plants for the greenhouse and there are others that need greenhouse cultivation entirely.

Some, such as the nasturtium, flower better if grown on rather poor soil. Most annuals will make too much leaf growth if grown in soil that is too rich or in shady places. Their rapid growth makes them invaluable for the new garden when flowers are wanted the first year, or for filling gaps in newly-planted herbaceous borders. Some, such as trail-

1 Nemesia strumosa, a half-hardy annual, has flowers in many colours.
2 'Yellow Pygmy' with double flowers is a useful variety of the tall annual Sunflower, Helianthus annuus.
3 Papaver somniferum, the Opium Poppy, is a hardy annual with single or fully double flowers.
4 The half-hardy Venidio-arctotis 'Tangerine' is one of the brightly-coloured varieties of this hybrid.
5 Linum grandiflorum, a hardy annual Flax, has flowers in scarlet, red or rose.
6 Thelesperma burridgeanum, a hardy annual from Texas, has yellow blooms with reddish-brown centres.

ing lobelias, dwarf nasturtiums and petunias are useful plants for hanging baskets. Many are useful for providing colour in urns, terrace pots, window boxes, tubs and other plant containers. Certain low-growing annuals find a place in carpet bedding schemes such as are still found in public parks. Although the purist may frown upon their use in this way, a few annuals are suitable for the rock garden.

A number of annuals have very fragrant flowers. Some have flowers or seed heads which may be dried for winter decoration indoors (see Everlasting flowers).

Some annuals, including a number of those used for carpet bedding, are grown for the sake of their colourful foliage.

Apart from removing faded flowers, keeping them weeded and staking the taller kinds of annuals need little attention, and they are a quick and inexpensive way to provide masses of summer colour, especially in a new garden.

Planting

Of all the operations that contribute to successful gardening, correct planting procedure is one of the most important. Digging a hole, pushing in the plant and hoping is not enough. Any gardener who does just this is doomed to constant disappointments.

Before the actual planting is carried out, careful preparation of the site is necessary, whether the project involved is an extensive border, the planting of a bedding scheme, or the tiniest pocket for an alpine plant. Beds, borders or planting holes should be deeply dug before planting. As far as beds and borders are concerned, full-scale trenching is best although nowadays, most busy gardeners settle for double-digging, or bastard trenching as it is sometimes called.

The surface soil must be broken down to a tilth of a fineness appropriate to the size of the specimens which are to be planted. Obviously, the ground for trees and shrubs will not require such careful preparation as it will for annual bedding plants or alpines.

As well as being thoroughly broken down, the soil should be in good heart. This means that it must contain enough humus and plant foods for the initial requirements of whatever is being planted. This can be achieved by digging in adequate quantities of humus-rich materials such as peat, leafmould, well rotted garden compost, or animal manures.

These can be supplemented by a dressing of a slow-acting organic fertiliser such as bonemeal or steamed bone flour, forked into the topsoil a week or

1 Peat is spread over the soil to a depth of 2 inches before planting begins.
2 The peat is forked lightly into the top few inches of soil.
3 Thorough raking is carried out before planting to prepare a fine tilth and remove stones. This is particularly important before small seedlings are set out, since the tender young roots need a minimum of resistance.

two in advance of planting or, where individual plantings are concerned, sprinkled into the holes.

Different kinds of plants will obviously need different planting procedures. The smaller they are, the more carefully should the operation be carried out. Appearances, however, can sometimes be deceptive. Nothing could look more delicate and vulnerable than a seedling that has just made its first pair of true leaves. And yet, at this stage—the best stage for planting out most seedlings—they can be surprisingly tough, perhaps because transplanting causes less damage to their rudimentary root system provided that they are transferred, without undue delay, from seed pans into boxes or nursery beds.

Seedlings should be handled gently, yet firmly, easing them carefully out of the seed compost and grasping them firmly by the leaves between thumb and forefinger as you plant them out in their new soil.

After this operation, particular attention should be paid to watering. Little and often is the rule to follow. Over-watering can cause damping-off, but seedlings should never be allowed to dry out completely; this can prove equally disastrous.

Planting annuals and bedding plants It is important to success when planting annuals, to ensure that they receive as little check as possible; they will then start into active growth again almost immediately. Whether plants come out of boxes, pots or nursery beds, it is always better to wait for a day when the soil is moist (but not soggy) after rain and when the atmosphere is humid. In these conditions, the plants will lose little moisture through transpiration.

If planting out time should coincide with a long dry spell, the only course is to soak both plants and planting holes with water a few hours in advance. The water should be allowed to drain away from the holes before the plants go in. As soon as the soil is friable and the weather favourable, hardy annuals should be sown where the plants are to flower. These quick growing plants are excellent for 'gapping' in a new herbaceous border where the perennials are still small. If the ground was not prepared last month, the area to be sown should be marked off with short sticks at once, the soil forked over and plenty of damp horticultural peat added to the top 2 or 3 inches. Soil for seed sowing needs to be very fine for good germination.

So the surface should be well raked down to a sand-like tilth before scattering the seed thinly, broadcast or in drills, just covered with soil. Twiggy sticks placed over the newly sown area will deter birds and prevent cats using the soil as a scratching ground.

Bedding plants should never be out of the ground for any length of time. They can suffer a serious check if they are left lying in the sun or in drying winds. The ideal course is to get them straight from box to bed. This is a difficulty that does not arise with plants that are set out from pots.

When planting from seed boxes, the roots of each individual plant should, if possible, be carefully disentangled from those of its neighbours. This will minimise damage and enable the plants to get away again quickly.

Some hardy annuals may be sown in August or September to flower early the following summer. As soon as the seedlings are large enough to handle they should be thinned. With autumn-sown annuals leave the final thinning until the following spring. Distances apart vary considerably, depending on the ultimate height of the annual, but as a general guide dwarf-growing annuals should be thinned to 4–6 inches apart. Those that grow to 15–18 inches tall should be thinned to 9–12 inches and taller kinds should be thinned to 1–2 feet apart.

If seed is wanted for sowing again next year it is best to mark a few good plants early in the summer. The seed-heads should not be gathered until they are fully ripe.

Half-hardy annuals Some annuals and a few perennials treated as annuals will not stand frost, so they are sown under glass in pots, pans or seed boxes, using seed compost or a soil-less seed compost. Sow the seeds thinly and cover and then place a sheet of glass and a piece of brown paper over the pot or box. Turn the glass daily to prevent condensation drips from falling on to the soil. Remove the paper as soon as the seeds germinate but leave the glass on for a further few days, tilting it slightly to admit some air.

When the seedlings are large enough prick them out into boxes of potting compost or a soil-less potting compost and shade them for a day or two from strong sunlight.

When watering seed boxes it is best to

immerse them in water up to their rims until all the compost is thoroughly damp. i.e., when the surface has darkened. This method is preferable to watering overhead. Where a soilless seed compost based on peat and sand is used the initial watering usually suffices.

It is essential to harden the plants off well before they are planted out into their flowering positions at the end of May or the beginning of June. Transfer the boxes to a cold frame and gradually increase the ventilation, eventually leaving the lights off altogether except on nights when frost is likely. If a frame is not available, gradually increase the greenhouse ventilation, finally leaving doors and vents open day and night.

It is a great mistake to sow too early under glass as this simply means that the plants receive a severe check by becoming over-crowded in their boxes while waiting to be planted out into their permanent positions.

The damping-off disease at the seedling stage can be troublesome but it can be controlled to a very large extent by using sterilized or soil-less composts and by watering with Cheshunt compound.

It is also possible to sow half-hardy annuals in the open ground in May or early June and, flowering later, they extend the flowering season.

Greenhouse annuals Many hardy, half-hardy and tender annuals make colourful plants for the cool greenhouse. They may also be grown in this way for cut flowers; or the pots, when in flower, may be taken into the house.

Seed is sown as for half-hardy annuals in pans, pots or boxes and the seedlings are potted up when they are large enough to handle. Pot-on as soon as the roots fill the pot. Some annuals resent being transplanted so it is best to sow these straight into their flowering pots and thin out the seedlings later.

The great advantage of a greenhouse for annuals is that flowers may be had throughout the year by sowing at different times. The temperature when sowing should be about 65°F (18°C), but it is not necessary to maintain this high temperature afterwards, provided the greenhouse is completely frost free. Many of the greenhouse annuals will need their growing points pinched out to encourage bushy plants and some will need staking. Water liberally in the summer months but moderately in the winter, and feed the plants with weak liquid manure at regular intervals.

Many seeds of annuals can be sown directly into patio pots to give vivid colour later in the year and spring is the time to sow them. Seed is generally so inexpensive and readily available that a few failures are of no major significance. Alyssum, candytuft, nigella, campanula, mignonette, Virginian stock, wallflowers, forget-me-nots, pansies, *Anemone japonica*, London pride, armeria, arabis and many others

1 For planting in restricted spaces, for example between stones in a dry wall, a narrow two-pronged fork is useful.
2 The best tool to use for preparing holes for small plants is the trowel. The use of a dibber is not recommended, as the roots may get caught in a pocket of air.
3 Firming every plant gently after transplanting is very important. Do not push too hard, as young roots are easily damaged, but ensure that no air pockets are trapped below the surface.

are suitable and effective.

Choose low-growing plants rather than tall and make sure always that they do not get too dry at the roots.

As in the open garden, the greatest

effect is to be obtained by planting colours in concentrated blocks rather than scattering them indiscriminately like confetti. Annuals are cheap and instantly effective, so here, according to colour groupings, are brief selections of low growing annuals suited to window-boxes as well as container plantings on patio, balcony and roof garden. Some flowers, of course, come in several different colours, so may be listed more than once.

White: alyssum, begonia, daisy, candy-tuft, *Celosia nana*, dianthus, echium, eschscholzia, forget-me-not, gazania, linaria, lobelia, mignonette, nemesia, nemophila, pansy, petunia, *Phlox drummondii*, polyanthus, portulaca, Virginian stock, verbena.

Yellow: *Celosia nana*, eschscholzia, gazania, leptosiphon, limnanthes, nasturtium, nemesia, pansy, polyanthus, *Tagetes signata*, wallflower.

Red: anagallis, begonia, *Dianthus sinensis*, eschscholzia, leptosiphon, mignonette, nasturtium, nemesia, petunia, *Phlox drummondii*, polyanthus, portulaca, *Silene pendula*, Virginian stock, verbena, wallflower.

Blue: anagallis, anchusa, echium, forget-me-not, lobelia, nemesia, nemophila, pansy, petunia, phacelia, polyanthus, Virginian stock, verbena, viscaria.

Choose boxes of plants which are showing colour but which also have many buds waiting to open. Inspect them carefully to ensure that there is no disease present and that the soil is moist. When you get them home keep them in a cool and shady spot until you are ready to plant them.

Have your containers ready with soil, either potting compost or one of the proprietary no-soil mixtures. Water the boxes of plants again a few minutes before planting and then lift each plant out carefully with a good ball of soil adhering to the roots. Plant with a trowel, spreading the roots well and firming the soil over them. Water again thoroughly until water begins to trickle from the drainage holes. Leave the newly planted containers in shade for a day or two before bringing them to their final positions.

Once the plants are growing away well, examine them each day for disease, water regularly and pick off all dead flowers to ensure a continuity of bloom. Any plant that dies should be removed at once, both for the appearance of the container and in case the dead or dying plant spreads its infection to its neighbours.

Cloches

There are certain flowers which are particularly suited to cloche cultivation. These can be brought into bloom several weeks earlier and the quality of the flower is often much better. Hardy annuals, in particular, are ideal plants for cloche protection during the early

1 In a window box planted for summer flowering, purple and white Petunias are used with deep scarlet Pelargoniums and white Oxeye Daisies. Trails of yellow Lysimachia nummularia hang down to cover the box.

2 For the best effect in boxes and pots, use summer flowering plants that are just coming into bloom, taking care not to injure the roots during transplanting.

stages of their growth. The most important of these are sweet peas.

Sweet Peas Sowing time for sweet peas in the north and south is late September. Seed can also be sown in March. The strip of ground should be deeply worked and plenty of organic matter incorporated in the form of peat, old manure or composted vegetable waste. Seed is sown one row per small cloche and two under the larger types. Space the seeds 6 inches apart in the rows. Cloches must be placed over the rows as soon as the seed is sown in the north. Southern sowings need not be covered until early October.

As soon as the plants are a few inches high, they should be provided with pieces of brushwood, through which they will grow. If large flowers are required, plants should be grown in the cordon system. Only the strongest side-growth is allowed to grow on after the initial stopping, and this growth should be trained up a strong cane. Plenty of water is required during the summer. There are so many beautiful, reliable varieties that a selection should be made from a specialist's catalogue.

Other hardy annuals Those suitable for cloche work and autumn sowing include calendula, candytuft, cornflower, scabious, viscaria, sweet sultan and nigella. For spring sowing the following are recommended: godetia, mignonette and clarkia. Seed is sown in groups as thinly as possible or in single rows. Large cloches can accommodate two rows.

Half-hardy annuals These benefit considerably from early covering after they have been sown in early April. Seed is sown thinly in single or double rows according to the size of the cloche. Final thinning is from 8-12 inches apart. Suitable varieties include zinnias, schizanthus, nemesia, nicotiana, petunia, and dimorphotheca.

Fragrant annuals

Those in search of fragrance are more likely to find it among the annuals and biennials than among the hardy perennials, for it is a quality possessed by many of the plants that are raised from seed sown in the spring, either under glass or in the open ground. Of these undoubtedly the most popular are the delightfully fragrant sweet peas, varieties of *Lathyrus odoratus*. As with other plants the fragrance varies a good deal but a good seedsman's list will make a point of describing those which possess it more strongly than others. Among other annuals and biennials which have it are Sweet Alison (*Lobularia maritima*), wallflowers (*cheiranthus*), snapdragons (*antirrhinum*), ten-week, Brompton and East Lothian stocks (*Matthiola incana*), night-scented stock (*Matthiola bicornis*), marigolds (*calendula*), nasturtiums (*tropaeolum*), mignonette (*Reseda odorata*), Sweet Sultan (*Centaurea moschata*), the sweet-scented tobacco plant (*nicotiana*), sweet scabious (*Scabiosa atropurpurea*), annual lupins and the biennial evening primrose (*Oenothera odorata*). All of these are popular with most gardeners, but less well known, perhaps, is the Marvel of Peru (*Mirabilis jalapa*), a half-hardy annual with small trumpet-shaped flowers in various colours, their fragrance identical with that of the sweet-scented tobacco plant. *Cleome spinosa*, the spider flower is another less common annual, 3 feet or so tall, with spidery-petalled pink or white flowers which add fragrance to their other attractions.

Bedding out

This term, in use by gardeners, describes a form of gardening in which plants raised elsewhere in a nursery garden or greenhouse are planted in a previously prepared bed.

The description bedding plant is not an exact one and only means that the plant is grown elsewhere in some quantity and then planted out as a temporary occupant of the bed; this being known as 'bedding out'.

The bedding plant in private gardens has, in general, had its day, since this style of gardening entails much expertise.

In public gardens and for certain formal occasions the bedding plant still has its uses.

Summer bedding Bedding plants for summer planting must be raised in early spring under glass. The skill of the operation is proved when a good uniform crop of plants is ready and hardened-off.

1 Cloche protection, given here to Polyanthus, insures speedy germination and improves the quality of the blooms. It also prevents damage by birds.
2 The fragrant flowers of the annual Evening Primrose open in the late afternoon and early evening and fill the garden with lovely scent.

Borders

There is no strict definition of the somewhat loose gardening feature known as a border, and there may, on occasions, become confusion between beds and borders. However, for the sake of convenience, a border may be looked upon as a bed which is considerably longer than it is wide. True beds are normally round, oval, square or rectangular, or of some other geometric shape in which the length is not much more than, perhaps, two or three times greater than the width, although even this cannot be considered to be an exact definition since a bed, say, 2 feet wide and 6–8 feet long would be better described as a bed rather than a border; longer than this it may be considered as a narrow border, sometimes described as a 'ribbon' border.

Two kinds of border which are occasionally seen, more often in large gardens than in small ones, are those devoted to one kind of plant and to plants of one colour. These can make pleasant features, but the drawback to a border devoted to one kind of plant is that its season is a short one. Thus a border planted up entirely with, say, lupins, paeonies, or delphiniums will be effective for not much more than three to four weeks. This may be tolerated in the large garden but is wasteful of space in smaller gardens. The one-colour border can be planned to have a much longer life, probably throughout much of the summer, but it is not easy to design to give continuity without awkward gaps appearing as plants go out of flower.

Another kind of border is the annual border, consisting entirely of hardy and half-hardy annuals. It is not too easy to plan a successful annual border, but properly planned and looked after it can be one of the most colourful features for many weeks during the summer and early autumn. When preparing the plan, which should be done on paper first, it is essential to take into consideration the differing heights of the plants to obtain a satisfactory overall effect, and their colours to avoid colour clashes, particularly as many of the more popular annuals tend to have bright colours, not all of which associate well together. The unfortunate visual effect which can be produced by grouping orange and the brighter reds together, can usually be avoided by separating these colours with patches of white-flowered plants or with grey-leaved annuals.

To prolong the flowering period as much as possible it is essential to deadhead the plants as soon as the flowers fade, otherwise they will run to seed and cease to flower. Regular feeding with weak liquid fertilizer will also help to make the plants flower longer.

The range of plants which may be grown is wide, with great variation in height and colour. It includes a fair number of plants grown for their colourful foliage. A pleasant effect, especially in a long, narrow border, may be obtained by using dwarf annuals only, those up to about 9 inches tall.

Another way of filling bare patches during the summer particularly, is to plunge pots of plants in flower into the ground, to their rims. Such plants as dahlias and early-flowering chrysanthemums may also be used to provide extra colour. The imaginative gardener will find still more variations of planting up the mixed border to provide a satisfactory and colourful feature.

All borders need extremely careful planning, and maintenance must be fairly consistent to keep the border at an optimum level of enjoyment. A complete overhaul is necessary during the dormant season, the time when the ground is dug thoroughly and fertilizer applied in preparation for the following year's blooming season. The annual border is a great advantage here; in other kinds of borders, mixed or devoted entirely to shrubs, bulbs or herbaceous plants, the plants remain in the ground and must be worked round with enormous care, which can be a time-consuming process.

1 Cladanthus arabicus, a plant from the western Mediterranean region, has yellow daisy-like flowers.
2 Tropaeolum majus is the well-known and deservedly popular Nasturtium.
3 A double-flowered form of the Pot Marigold, Calendula officinalis.
4 and 5 Two forms of the Californian Poppy, Eschscholzia californica, a hardy annual available in a wide choice of colours.

BIENNIALS

Biennials are a valuable division of garden plants for by the biennial habit of storing up in the first season a reserve which is expended wholly in the second season, a much greater quantity of blossom is possible than with either the annual or perennial habit of growth.

Where a new garden is being made annual and biennial plants will be of great service for it generally takes from three to five years to achieve a garden furnished satisfactorily with perennials and shrubs; and even then biennials will still be needed.

The chief drawback to the cultivation of biennials is the space which must be given to them in the reserve garden or frame, since they are not moved into their final stations until they are large, healthy plants.

The term *biennial* is not used too strictly by the gardener and some short-lived perennials, some monocarpic plants, and certain annuals also are sometimes given biennial treatment.

As with annuals, biennial plants are sub-divided into hardy and half-hardy biennials.

Cultivation Biennials may be sown in spring in a frame or cold greenhouse or outdoors from May onwards.

If seeds are sown in drills instead of broadcast it will be easier to keep them free from weeds by running the hoe between the rows from time to time.

After a severe thinning seedlings should be pushed on with adequate feeding until by October they will be large leafy plants, which may then be put into their final stations in the flower border. If the weather is dry when the time comes to transplant give the bed a thorough watering. Careful lifting, using a trowel, will minimize root disturbance, and subsequent checks to growth.

If it is intended to treat hardy annuals as biennials (and this gives excellent results) the only way in which the operation differs from that described above is in the time of the seed sowing, which should be at the end of the summer or even in early autumn, but do not sow too early or the plants will flower in their first year. Given this biennial treatment, annuals will make much larger plants than when grown in the normal way and this must be allowed for when they are planted out in their final positions.

Half-hardy biennials will need over-wintering in frost-free conditions in a frame or a cold greenhouse. They are not an important section and one may well do without them, devoting precious greenhouse space to other things.

The following are biennials, or are often treated as biennial: adlumia, althaea (hollyhock), antirrhinum (snapdragon), *Campanula medium* (Canterbury bell), cheiranthus (wallflower), cnicus (fishbone thistle), *Dianthus barbatus* (Sweet William), *Digitalis purpurea* (foxglove), *Erysimum arkansanum*, *Hedysarum coronarium* (French honeysuckle), *Humea elegans* (half-hardy), hunnemannia, lunaria (honesty), matthiola (Brompton, Nice and Intermediate stock), some meconopsis, myosotis, *Oenothera biennis* (evening primrose), onopordon (cotton thistle), *Papaver nudicaule* (Iceland poppy), verbascum (mullein).

1 Dianthus barbatus, the well-known Sweet William, and 2, Lunaria biennis, the Honesty, are two of the many plants known as biennials, sown one year to flower the next.

Nigella 'Persian Jewels'

Ageratum (aj-er-a-tum)

From the Greek *a*, not, *geras*, old, a reference to the non-fading flowers (*Compositae*). Floss flower. Half-hardy compact annuals from Mexico. Useful for summer bedding schemes, carpeting, edging and window boxes. The English name floss flower well describes the blue-mauve tassel-like flowers borne in fluffy heads, which last well.

Species cultivated *A. houstonianum* (syn. *A. mexicanum*) 1½ feet when grown naturally. Heart-shaped leaves in rosette formation. Cultivars include 'Florist Blue', 'Little Dorrit' azure blue, 'Mexican White', 'Fairy Pink', 'Blue Ball'.

Cultivation Ageratums like a sunny spot and need to be planted not less than 6 inches apart to be effective. Propagation is by seed sown in pans in March in a temperature of 55°F (13°C). Prick off, and about ten days later pinch out the tips of the shoots to ensure branched and compact specimens. Harden off and plant out in late May or early June. The flowering season will be prolonged if the dead flower-heads are removed from time to time. When a really good colour is obtained cuttings may be taken in spring from a plant that has been potted up in the late summer and flower-buds removed. Pot up and harden off once the cuttings have rooted and plant out in May.

Alonsoa (al-on-so-a)

Named after a Spanish official, Alonzo Zanoni (*Scrophulariaceae*). Mask Flower. Half-hardy shrubby perennials with racemes of flowers. Grown as annuals outside or as perennials under glass.

Species cultivated *A. acutifolia* 1½–2 feet, bushy in habit, scarlet flowers; var. *alba*, white June outside or winter under glass. Both good as greenhouse pot plants or as half-hardy annuals. *A. incisifolia*, 1–2 feet, shrubby, for greenhouse cultivation, scarlet flowers, summer. *A. linearis*, to 2 feet, shrubby, grown as annual or greenhouse perennial, scarlet flowers, May–October; var. *gracilis*, more slender. *A. meridionalis* (syn. *A. mutisii*), 1 foot, flowers dull orange, summer.

Cultivation Recommended compost: 2 parts of loam, 1 of leaf mould and 1 of coarse sand. Plants require a sunny position under glass or outside and only moderate watering. Pot in March. Minimum winter temperature: 50°F (10°C). Propagation is by seed sown in March at 60°F (16°C), or by cuttings in August.

Alyssum

From the Greek *a*, not, and *lyssa*, madness: once thought to cure madness or rage (*Cruciferae*). Madwort. The dwarf perennial species in cultivation, mostly with grey foliage and yellow flowers, are chiefly confined to the rock garden; the taller-growing kinds are best in borders. The popular sweet alyssum or sweet Alison, is now correctly called *Lobularia maritima*.

Species cultivated *A. alpestre*, 3 inches, of tufted habit, flowering in June. *A. argenteum*, to 18 inches, becomes woody at the base. Deep yellow flowers in clustered heads, May–July. *A. flexicaule*, 3 inches, tufts of fragrant yellow flowers, spring. *A. idaeum*, of trailing habit, soft yellow flowers, May–June. *A. moellendorfianum*, 6 inches, silvery plant, flowers in long racemes. *A. montanum*, to 10 inches, usually much lower, fragrant flowers, bright yellow, in loose racemes. *A. pyrenaicum*, 8–10 inches, dwarf shrubby growth, white velvety leaves, white flowers, summer. *A. saxatile*, gold dust, to 12 inches, spreading habit, numerous heads of golden-yellow flowers, April–June, vars. *citrinum*, lemon-yellow, *compactum*, 4–6 inches, 'Dudley Neville', 6–9 inches, biscuit yellow, *plenum*, double flowers, dwarf, 'Tom Thumb', *variegatum*, variegated foliage, yellow and green. *A. wulfenianum*, 3 inches, round, thick, silver leaves, pale yellow flowers in large, loose heads borne in summer.

Cultivation Alyssums require only ordinary, well-drained soils in the open. *A. saxatile* is often grown vertically in walls or on banks. It should be trimmed back after flowering to prevent it from straggling unduly. Young plants are occasionally used in spring bedding schemes. Propagation is by seed, division or by 2–3 inch long cuttings taken in early summer and rooted in shade.

Amaranthus (am-a-ran-thus)

So named (from the Greek *a*, not, and *maraino*, to fade) because of the lasting qualities of the flowers (*Amaranthaceae*). Half-hardy annuals grown in sub-tropical bedding schemes, some for their coloured foliage, in shades of red, crimson and green. They are good for pot culture under glass. *A. caudatus*, love-lies-bleeding, and *A. hypochondriacus*, prince's feather, are two of the hardiest and can be treated as hardy annuals in warmer areas.

Species cultivated *A. caudatus*, 2–3 feet, long, red, drooping tail-like flowers, August; vars. *albiflorus*, greenish white, *atropurpureus*, blood red. *A. gibbosus*, dwarf, slender flowers in red clusters. *A. hypochondriacus*, 4–5 feet, flowers in dense spikes, deep crimson, July, purplish green foliage; vars. *atropurpureus*, dark, *sanguineus*, blood red throughout, *sanguineus nanus*, dwarf form, *splendens*, good crimson foliage. *A. melancholicus*, 1–3 feet, grown chiefly for its variable coloured foliage; vars. *ruber*, leaves crimson, *bicolor*, leaves green streaked yellow, *tricolor*, Joseph's coat, 18 inches, purple and green leaves, yellow stalks, *salicifolius*, 3 feet, narrow, brightly coloured leaves, bronze-green with orange and crimson markings. Cultivars: 'Fire King', 'Molten Torch', 'Pygmy Torch'.

1 Ageratum houstonianum is a half-hardy annual used for summer bedding. 2 Alonsoa meridionalis, the Mask Flower, is a half-hardy shrubby perennial usually grown as an annual in the open garden.

Cultivation Plant out in June in sunny beds. Propagate by seed sown in a temperature of 55–60°F (13–16°C) in March. Harden off young plants carefully before planting out.

Amellus (a-mel-us)

From the name given by Virgil to a similar flower growing by the River Mella (*Compositae*). A small genus of annual or perennial plants from South Africa, easily grown, requiring no special care. They have single daisy-like flowers.

Species cultivated *A. annuus* (syn. *Kaulfussia amelloides*), 6 inches, yellow-centred blue flowers about 3–4 inches across, summer. An annual. *A. lychnitis*, 6 inches, an evergreen trailing plant with violet flower heads.

Cultivation *A. annuus* is grown as a hardy annual, propagated by seed sown in spring. *A. lychnitis* is a greenhouse perennial pot plant, increased by division or by cuttings from new growth in spring.

Ammobium (am-o-be-um)

Derived from Greek words *ammos*, sand and *bio*, to live, describing its sandy habitat (*Compositae*). Everlasting sand flower. The single species available is particularly useful as an 'everlasting' cut flower. It is normally grown as a half-hardy annual, though September-sown seedlings can be raised in a cool greenhouse. *A. alatum* grows 18–24 inches tall and its flower-heads are

1 The lemon-yellow Alyssum saxatile citrinum are excellent plants for a dry wall or a sunny bank.
2 Amaranthus 'Molten Torch' and 3 Amaranthus caudatus, Love-lies-Bleeding, are two half-hardy annuals used in sub-tropical bedding schemes.

silvery-white and yellow, about 1 inch across, var. *grandiflorum* has larger flowerheads, 2 inches across, summer.

Cultivation Seed is usually raised under glass in a temperature of 50–55°F (10–15°C), in early spring. Plant out in May at 6 inches apart in rich, light soil in a warm spot. Alternatively seed may be sown outside direct into borders in May; or, as above, in September to obtain larger plants. Flowers will remain their true silver-white colour if cut before they are fully expanded and hung up-sidedown in an airy building in shade.

Anagallis (an-a-gal-is)

From the Greek *anagelao*, meaning delightful (*Primulaceae*). Pimpernel. Though some species are naturally perennials, it is usual to treat all as annuals in cultivation. As such they are a delight at the front of the annual border, as they are usually low or even trailing in habit. *A. tenella* may be used to great advantage in a moist or boggy spot.

Species cultivated *A. arvensis* (poor man's weather glass), of prostrate growth, flowers $\frac{1}{4}$ inch wide, variable shades between scarlet and white, late summer; vars. *caerulea*, blue; *phoenicea*, red; *latifolia*, blue. *A. linifolia*, 12 inches, flowers blue, red undersides, $\frac{1}{2}$ inch wide, July; vars. *breweri*, red, *collina*, flowers rosy purple; *lilacina*, lilac; *monellii*, flowers larger than the species; *phillipsii*, deep gentian-blue. *A. tenella* (bog pimpernel), 2–4 inches, bell-shaped flowers, $\frac{1}{2}$ inch across, pink with darker veins, summer.

Cultivation A sunny spot suits these charming plants, in ordinary garden soil; a moist place for *A. tenella*. Seed may either be sown in heat in March and planted out in June, or sown direct into flowering positions in April. *A. linifolia* may be propagated by division in March if kept as a perennial.

Antirrhinum (an-tir-i-num)

From the Greek, *anti*, like, *rhinos*, snout, a reference to the curiously shaped flowers (*Scrophulariaceae*). The most important of these nearly hardy perennials is the snapdragon, *Antirrhinum majus*, which is grown extensively as a half-hardy annual for bedding purposes. In some districts it will prove hardy and remain perennial but as the plants are inclined to become straggly after the first year they are nearly always treated as annuals, although plants are sometimes naturalised in the crannies of old walls. *A. majus* originally came from the Mediterranean region where it grows to 3 feet in height. It has been considerably developed for bedding purposes by plant breeders. Species suitable for the rock garden are *A. asarina* and *A. glutinosum*, but like *A. majus* they are not reliably hardy.

Species cultivated *A. asarina*, a trailing plant with yellow flowers, from June to

1

2

3

1 *Anagallis linifolia is one of the best of the blue-flowered annuals.*
2 *Antirrhinum 'Sentinel Sunlight'.*
3 *The South African Amellus annuus has blue flowers with yellow centres.*

September. *A. glutinosum*, low growing with yellow and cream flowers in summer. *A. majus*, 3 feet, the well-known snapdragon. Flowers pink in the species. Many garden forms have developed from this species by natural variation. It has also been hybridized to produce plants in a wide range of colours and of various heights including dwarf spreading plants. Plants remain in flower over a long period, through summer and autumn.

Some good cultivars *Tall* (3–4 feet): 'Cloth of Gold', golden yellow. 'Giant Ruffled Tetra' strain mixed colours, large. 'Rocket Hybrids', mixed large flowers, vigorous plants. *Intermediate* (1½ feet): 'Dazzler' brilliant scarlet. 'Eldorado', deep, rich golden yellow. 'Fire King', orange and white. 'Malmaison', silver pink, dark foliage, 'Orange Glow', deep orange, cerise throat, 'Purity' white. Regal Rose', an F.1 rust-resistant hybrid; rich rose red. *Dwarf* (9 inches); 'Floral Carpet' Mixed F.1 Hybrids, extremely colourful. 'Magic Carpet Strain' mixed colours. 'Tom Thumb', 9 inches, available in various colours or mixed. *Rust resistant:* 'Amber Monarch', golden amber. 'Orange Glow', deep orange, cerise throat. 'Rust Resistant Roselight', rich glowing salmon, 'Toreador', deep crimson. 'Victory', buff pink, suffused orange. 'Wisley Golden Fleece', yellow. Seedsmen list many more and new ones appear regularly.

Cultivation The low growing species, *A. asarina* and *A. glutinosum*, need plenty of sun and good drainage and may be planted in April in any ordinary soil. It is wise to take cuttings in August, inserting them in sandy soil in a pot in case the parent plants are killed by frost in the winter. The garden forms of *A. majus* grown as half-hardy annuals, are sown in March in a temperature of 70°F (21°C); the seedlings are pricked out into boxes and then hardened off and planted out in May or the beginning of June. They may be used to fill gaps in borders but look best when planted in drifts in the garden or in bedding displays in public parks. Seed may also be sown outdoors in April. Plants may also be grown in pots in the cool greenhouse for spring display, for which purpose seed is sown in August. Plenty of ventilation should be given at all times. The height of these snapdragons varies a great deal, from the 9 inches of the dwarf kinds to the 4 feet of the tall varieties. Under glass, in pots, the latter may, by careful feeding and attention to watering, be induced to grow even taller.

A great deal of hybridizing has been carried out with these popular bedding plants and there are now tetraploid cultivars which have larger flowers on robust plants.

Antirrhinum rust is a troublesome disease of cultivated snapdragons caused by the attack of one of the rust fungi known as *Puccinia antirrhini*. It

Antirrhinum majus 'Fiery Red' is a tall growing perennial usually cultivated as an annual.

shows first as light brown pustules on the under surface of the leaves and later there appear dark brown ones on leaves and stems. Even small seedlings can be infected. Spraying may be useful if repeated often, but the only real remedy is to grow resistant varieties.

Arctotis (ark-to-tis)

From *arktos*, a bear in Greek and *ous*, an ear, probably referring to the shaggy fruits of this annual (*Compositae*). Decorative half-hardy annuals and pernnials, mostly from South Africa, that flower from July to September and like being baked in the sun on a warm sunny bank.

Annual species cultivated *A. breviscapa*, 6 inches, orange. *A. grandis*, 1½ feet, silvery flowers with blue reverse. *A. laevis*, 8 inches, flowers brownish, suffused red. *A. stoechadifolia*, 2 feet, flowers white, blue reverse.

Parennial species cultivated *A. acaulis*, 6 inches, orange-carmine.

Hybrids There are large-flowered hybrids, half-hardy annuals listed as *A. × hybrida*, in a wide colour range, including yellows, oranges, reds, crimsons, purples and whites. All are about 1–1½ feet tall. 'Crane Hill', 2 feet, has white flowers with a blue centre and a yellow zone (see also Venidio-Arctotis).

Cultivation Sow seeds in heat in March, prick out the seedlings and harden them off before planting them out 1 foot apart when frosts are over. They make excellent plants for the unheated greenhouse in pots containing loam and leafmoud in equal parts, plus a little sharp sand. These should start in a sunny place and should be watered moderately from October to March, freely at other times. Cuttings may be taken in early summer and rooted and overwintered in a frame or greenhouse, but propagation by seed is the usual method. *A. acaulis* needs cloche or frame protection in winter.

Argemone (ar-gem-o-ne)
From the Greek *argemos*, meaning a white spot, referring to a cataract on the eye which this plant was said to cure (*Papaveraceae*). A small genus of hardy summer-flowering perennial plants from America with poppy-like flowers, usually grown as annuals.

Species cultivated *A. grandiflora*, 3 feet, flowers large, up to 4 inches across, white, satiny lustre, leaves thistle-like, white-veined; var. *lutea*, yellow flowers. *A. mexicana*, prickly poppy, devil's fig, 2 feet, annual with spiny foliage, flowers 2½ inches across, lemon-yellow or orange. *A. platyceras*, 1–4 feet, white or purple flowers.

Cultivation The argemones do well in sandy soils and sunny situations. Sow the seeds in April thinly, where they are to flower, and thin later, spacing the plants 9 inches apart. They may also be grown from seed sown under glass in spring. The seedlings are pricked off into individual small pots and planted out in the open in May after they have been hardened off.

Arnebia (ar-ne-be-a)
Arneb, the Arabic name for one of the species gives this genus its name (*Boraninaceae*). Annuals and perennials that have been introduced from Turkey and Armenia, among them the prophet flower.

Species cultivated *A. cornuta*, 1½–2 feet, an annual, flowers yellow with purplish-brown spots in summer. *A. echioides*, 1 foot, the prophet flower, yellow flowers in summer, marked with brownish-purple spots, a perennial.

Cultivation Plant the perennial species in autumn or spring and propagate by seeds or division in spring. Sow seeds of the annuals in a frame or cool greenhouse in March and plant out seedlings in May. They all like an open, well-drained position and are not particular as to soil.

Asperula (as-per-u-la)
From the Greek *asper*, rough, as the leaves are rough to touch (*Rubiaceae*). A genus of herbaceous perennials and annuals, and a few shrubs, for the rock and woodland garden.

Species cultivated *A. arcadiensis*, low growing, deep pink tubular flowers, spring, needs protection against damp in winter. *A. gussonii*, 1 inch, forms low cushions and has shell-pink flowers in spring. *A. hexaphylla*, 1 foot, white flowers in summer. *A. lilaciflora caespitosa*,

prostrate form, pink flowers, a plant for the scree. *A. odorata*, the native woodruff, 9 inches, white, very fragrant flowers in spring, does well in shade. *A. orientalis*, 1 foot, annual with very fragrant blue flowers, summer. *A. suberosa*, makes an extensive 3 inch high mound smothered with pink flowers in summer, needs winter protection against damp, a good plant for the alpine house. *A. tinctoria*, prostrate, white flowers, summer.

Cultivation The perennial species, except where indicated, need well-drained soil and sunny positions. All may be propagated by seed and some of the perennial species will divide quite easily although *A. suberosa* and *A. arcadiensis* are more difficult. The annual *A. orientalis* thrives in a moist, shady position.

1 The blue flowers of Asperula orientalis are very fragrant.
2 An Arctotis hybrid.
3 A flower of Arctotis grandis.

1

2
3

Begonia (be-go-ne-a)

Commemorating Michel Bégon, 1638–1710, Governor of Canada, patron of botany (*Begoniaceae*). These half-hardy herbaceous and sub-shrubby plants are natives of moist tropical countries, apart from Australia. They need greenhouse treatment, though a large number are now used in summer bedding schemes.

The genus begonia is usually divided into two groups; those species with fibrous roots and those with tubers. Other classifications give special treatment to the winter-flowering forms, and to those grown exclusively for the interest of their leaves. A notable feature of begonias is their oblique, lop-sided leaves.

There has been so much hybridising in this genus that the naming has become quite complicated, and the custom of giving Latin specific names has not made matters easier.

The begonia, unlike the majority of plants, has, instead of hermaphrodite blooms, separate male and female blossoms on the same plant; the female flowers are generally removed as not being of much interest, though if seed is required,

1 and 2 Two excellent examples of large-flowered double begonia hybrids.
3 'Flamingo' is one of a number of Begonia semperflorens often used for summer bedding.
4 The Rex Begonias are grown for their colourful leaves.

they must, of course, be retained. The seed is dust-fine and needs no covering of soil, in fact the raising of begonias from seed has something in common with the art of raising ferns from spores.

Species cultivated The best-known begonias are the hybrids of the tuberous species: *B. boliviensis*, *B. clarkei*, *B. cinnabarina*, *B. davisii*, *B. pearcei*.

Another important group consists of the hybrids and varieties of *B. rex*, a plant from Assam with most interesting, colourful foliage. The winter-flowering and fibrous-rooted varieties derived from *B.* 'Gloire de Lorraine', a variety originally raised in France in 1891 by the plant breeder Victor Lemoine, who crossed *B. socotrana* and *B. dregei*, form a most valuable group as they furnish the greenhouse at a difficult time of the year.

Fibrous-rooted species include: *B. acutifolia*, white, spring. *B. angularis*, white-veined leaves. *B. coccinea*, scarlet, winter. *B. evansiana*, pink, almost hardy (possibly hardy in the south-west). *B. fuchsioides*, scarlet, winter. *B. froebelli*, scarlet, winter. *B. foliosa*, white and rose, summer. *B. glaucophylla*, pink and pendulous, winter. *B. haageana*, pink, autumn. *B. hydrocotylifolia*, pink, summer. *B. incarnata*, rose, winter. *B. manicata*, pink, winter. *B. scharffiana*, white, winter. *B. semperflorens*, rose (has important large-flowered vars.). *B. socotrana*, pink, winter.

Nurserymen's catalogues contain long lists of hybrids of the above, too numerous to mention here, but in various shades of pink, red, cream and white with enormous double flowers in a number of different forms.

Species with ornamental leaves include: *B. albo-picta*, *B. argenteo-guttata*, white and pink speckled leaves. *B. heracleifolia*, leaves deeply lobed. *B. imperialis*, velvety-green leaves. *B. boeringiana*, foliage purplish and green. *B. maculata*, foliage spotted white. *B. masoniana*, ('Iron Cross'), leaves green with a prominent dark 'iron cross' marking, popular as a houseplant. *B. metallica*, foliage has metallic lustre. *B. olbia*, bronze leaves spotted white. *B. rex*, foliage metallic silver and purple. *B. ricinifolia*, bronze leaves. *B. sanguinea*, leaves blood-red beneath. There are, in addition to the species given, many hybrids with beautiful leaves, especially named garden hybrids derived from *B. rex* and its varieties and other species, all known as Rex begonias.

Cultivation The fibrous-rooted begonias are usually obtained from seed, which should be sown in January in a temperature of 60°F (16°C). It is also possible to root growths from the base of the plant. The sub-shrubby perennial forms will

1 Begonia fuchsioides produces its scarlet flowers in winter in the greenhouse.
2 'Lady Roberts' is a large-flowered hybrid which blooms in winter.

come easily from normal cuttings, or all begonias may be raised by leaf cuttings. Leaf cuttings are single leaves which are pegged down in sandy compost, the undersides of all the main veins having been nicked with a razor blade. The temperature should be around 60–70°F (16–21°C). Little plants should form where veins were cut, and these may later be detached and potted-on separately. Most begonias need a winter temperature of about 60°F (16°C). The ornamental Rex type must not be exposed to full sunlight, and many of the other classes will be happy with much less light than suits other greenhouse plants.

The tuberous begonias may, of course, be grown from tubers. These are usually started into growth by placing them in shallow boxes of peat or leafmould in February or March, hollow side uppermost, in a temperature of 60–70°F (16–21°C). After roots have formed the tubers are potted up in small pots and later moved into larger ones. A compost of equal parts of loam, leafmould, well-rotted manure and silver sand is suitable. Do not start to feed these tuberous plants till they have formed roots, or they will decay, but after they are rooted a bi-weekly dose of liquid manure is helpful. The tuberous begonias may also

1 'Mrs Heal' is another winter-flowering Begonia.
2 Brachycome 'Purple King' is a striking hybrid of the Swan River Daisy.
3 Browallia speciosa is a handsome pot plant or annual bedding plant.

be raised from seed, and if this is sown in February plants may flower from July to October. These seed-raised plants are popular for summer bedding.

Tuberous begonias when their season is over must be gradually dried out. They may be left in their pots in a frost-proof shed, or knocked-out and stored in clean dry sand.

Brachycome (brak-e-ko-me)
From the Greek *brachys*, short, *comus*, hair (*Compositae*). A genus of half-hardy Australian annual or perennial herbs. The species usually cultivated is *B. iberidifolia*, the Swan River daisy, which grows 9–12 inches tall and has 1 inch wide daisy flowers in shades of blue, pink and white in summer. Named hybrids in separate colours are available, including: 'Little Blue Star', 'Purple King' and 'Red Star'.
Cultivation These plants are easily grown in a dry, sunny bed. Sow seed under glass in March in boxes of light soil and plant out in May, or sow in the open in early May where the plants are to flower. When sown under glass in August or September they will make good pot plants for early spring display under glass.

Browallia (brow-al-le-a)
Commemorating either Johan Browallius, Bishop of Abs, or Dr John Browall of Sweden (*Solanaceae*). Annual and perennial plants from South America, usually grown as greenhouse plants. In a sheltered garden the annual species may be bedded out in early June.
Species cultivated *B. americana* (syn. *B.*

demissa, B. elata), 1–1½ feet, soft violet-blue, June to October, annual. *B. grandiflora*, 2 feet, blue with yellow tube, July, annual, Peru. *B. speciosa*, 1½–2 feet, blue, violet or white, perennial greenhouse plant usually grown as an annual, Colombia. *B. viscosa*, 1–1½ feet, violet-blue, white centre, summer, perennial in the greenhouse.

Cultivation Sow the seed in March in finely sifted soil, only just covering it, and germinate in a temperature of 55–65°F (13–18°C). When large enough to handle transplant three or four seedlings to a 5 inch pot and stand the pots on the greenhouse shelf. Give weak manure; water during May and June. Pinch plants back to make them bushy. They will flower from July onwards. Seedlings for planting outdoors must be well hardened off before planting in June.

Calandrinia (kal-an-drin-e-a)

Commemorating J. L. Calandrini, a Swiss botanist (*Portulacaceae*). Some of the species of the rock purslane are perennial in their South American and Californian habitats but are usually treated as half-hardy annuals. They are useful for the rock garden or for sunny crevices. The colours are dazzling.

Species cultivated *C. grandiflora*, 1–1½ feet, rosy-red, July to October, fleshy foliage. *C. menziesii* (syn. *C. speciosa*), 6–9 inches, ruby-crimson, June to September. There is also a white variety. *C. umbellata*, 6 inches, magenta, July to September, leaves dark green, narrow. In mild areas this Peruvian species may survive outdoors for two or three years.

Cultivation Sow the seed in boxes in March at a temperature of 55–60°F (13–16°C). The soil should be light and well-drained. Transplant seedlings into small pots when large enough to handle and plant out in the open in June. The seed may also be sown out of doors in April where plants are to flower. The plants must have a sunny position, for the flowers need sun to open fully.

Calceolaria (kal-see-o-lair-e-a)

From the Latin *calceolus*, a slipper or little shoe, referring to the curious shape of the flower (*Scrophulariaceae*). Half-hardy and greenhouse plants, shrubby, herbaceous and rock garden plants. They are mostly natives of Chile and Peru.

Herbaceous species cultivated *C. amplexicaulis*, 1–2 feet, yellow, summer. *C. arachnoidea*, 9–12 inches, purple, June to September. *C. corymbosa*, 1–1½ feet, yellow and purple, May to October. *C. pavonii*, 3–5 feet, deep yellow and brown,

1 The dwarf Peruvian Calandrinia umbellata reaches 6 inches in height and flowers in late summer.
2 Callistephus chinensis, the China Aster, are half-hardy and will flourish in most soils in open, sunny positions.

Calendulas, sometimes called Marigolds, are hardy annuals growing 12 to 15 inches in height.
1 'Geisha Girl' is a cultivar with incurved blooms.
2 'Art Shades' is a double strain vastly superior to those with single blooms.

summer. *C. purpurea*, 1–2 feet, reddish-violet, July to September.

Hardy *C. acutifolia*, often confused with *C. polyrrhiza*, creeping, large yellow flowers with red dots, June. *C. biflora* (syn. *C. plantaginea*), 1 foot, yellow, July. *C. darwinii*, 3 inches, yellow with large brown spots on lip, June and July, rock garden or in a large pot in a cold frame; a difficult plant. *C. fothergillii*, 6 inches, sulphur-yellow, red spots, July. *C. tenella*, 3 inches, golden-yellow, crimson spots, June.

Cultivation: Herbaceous varieties Sow seed in July on the surface of fine soil in well-drained pans or shallow boxes. Cover with a sheet of glass and stand in a cold frame or under a bell-glass and keep moist and shaded. Transplant seedlings in August. In September pot singly into 2 inch pots in a compost of 2

parts of sandy loam, 1 part of leaf-mould, old manure and sharp sand. The winter temperature should be about 50°F (10°C). Discard the plants after they have flowered.

Hardy varieties Plant in March or September in soil enriched with leafmould and in partially shaded places on the rock garden. Water freely during dry weather in summer. Seed of annual varieties may be sown in the open during March and April.

Propagation of shrubby varieties is by cuttings 3 inches long inserted in sandy soil in a shaded cold frame in September or October, or in a cool greenhouse; hardy varieties by division of the roots in March, or by seed sown in pans in February or March and only very lightly covered with sifted soil. Place in a cold greenhouse or frame.

Calendula (kal-en-du-la)

From the Latin *calendae*, the first day of the month, probably referring to the fact that some species flower almost perpetually (*Compositae*). Natives of Europe. One species only is widely grown, *C. officinalis*, the English, or pot marigold; the latter name is derived from its use in the past as a herb for flavouring soups etc. The specific name *officinalis* also means it was once considered to have medicinal properties. A hardy annual, the species grows 12–15 inches tall and bears single, orange, daisy-like flowers on branching stems. Through hybridization there are now many attractive cultivars from cream to deep orange, double, semi-double and quilled, mainly taller than the type, reaching about 2 feet, and blooming continuously throughout the summer and early autumn.

Cultivars 'Art Shades', a strain in apricot, orange, cream, etc.; 'Campfire', deep orange, long stems; 'Crested mixed', various colours; 'Flame Beauty'; 'Geisha Girl', like an incurved chrysanthemum; 'Indian Maid', pale orange, maroon centre; 'Pacific Beauty mixed', large flowers, various shades; 'Radio', quilled; 'Rays of Sunshine', various colours; 'Twilight', cream.

Cultivation Any ordinary soil which is not too rich is suitable and though plants will bloom in the shade, they tend to become leggy, and a sunny site is best. Seed is sown thinly out of doors in March or April where plants are to flower and the seedlings thinned to 9 inches apart. Seed may also be sown in September, slightly more thickly. The seedlings are then left to stand the winter and thinned in the spring. Losses occur more through wet and cold winds than hard frosts, so choose a sheltered site and well-drained soil. Grown this way plants are useful for cloching if wished.

Callistephus (kal-is-tef-us)

From the Greek *kallistos*, most beautiful *stephos*, a crown, a reference to the flower (*Compositae*). A genus of a single species, introduced from China by a Jesuit missionary in 1731. This is *C. chinensis*, commonly known as the China or annual aster, a half-hardy annual. The original plants had single purple flowers on 2 foot stems but *C. chinensis* has been greatly hybridised to give a wide variety of flower form, in which the petals may be quilled, shaggy, plumed or neat. Colours range from white through pinks and reds to purples and blues and recently yellow has been introduced; heights vary from 6 inches to 2½ feet.

Among the most important are the wilt-resistant strains. These flowers may be used for exhibition, bedding, cut-flowers and some strains make useful pot plants.
Cultivation China asters grow on a wide range of soils provided they have been well cultivated and manured and the lime content maintained. Open sunny sites give best results. Seed is sown in March in a temperature of 55°F (13°C), and the seedlings subsequently pricked out and hardened off, for planting out in May. Seed may also be sown as late as April in the cold frame. Plant out 6–12 inches apart according to the height of the variety. When flower buds show, give a feed of weak liquid manure. Never allow the plants to receive a check in any way. When raising plants keep them growing the whole time.

Many new cultivars may be bought in separate colours, and several are wilt-resistant. A good seedsman's catalogue should be consulted.

Named strains, in mixed colours include:

Single flowered, all 2–2½ feet: 'Southcote Beauty', long petals; 'Super Chinensis', good for cutting; 'Upright Rainbow', attractive mixture of colours.

. Semi-double and double, dwarf: 'Bedder' series, 6 inches; 'Feather Cushion', 6 inches; 'Thousand Wonders', 6 inches; 'Dwarf Cartmel', wilt-resistant, 10 inches; 'Dwarf Chrysanthemum-Flowered', 12 inches; 'Dwarf Queen', 12 inches; 'Dwarf Waldersee', carpet effect, semi-double, wilt-resistant; 'Lilliput', 15 inches, cut-flower.

Early-flowering: 'Early Burpeeana', 18 inches; 'Early Curlylocks', 18 inches, ostrich plume type; 'Early Wonder', 15 inches, comet type; 'Queen of the Market', 2 feet, cut-flower.

From 2–3 feet: 'Bouquet Powderpuff', densely petalled, centre quilled; 'Californian Giants', good for exhibition; 'Comet', mid season, curling petals; 'Crego', branching, long-stemmed, fluffy appearance; 'Duchesse', American introduction, vigorous, inward curving like a chrysanthemum, includes yellow; 'Mammoth Victoria', bedding and cutting; 'Ostrich Plume', old favourite, now with wilt-resistant varieties; 'Paeony-flowered', incurved, pale colours; 'Rayonantha', new, quilled, wilt-resistant; 'Super Princess', similar to 'Bouquet Powderpuff'.

Celosia (se-lo-se-a)
From the Greek *kelos*, burnt, referring to the burnt appearance of the flowers of

The Celosias are a group of half-hardy annuals resembling fluffy grasses.
1 The flowers of Celosia plumosa, the Cockscomb, reach 18 inches and are produced in pyramidal, often drooping, panicles.
2 This red Cockscomb with contrasting bronze foliage is sometimes used on its own in the open garden.

1 Chrysanthemum segetum is a hardy annual that grows to about 18 inches in height.
2 Cheiranthus are treated as biennials by sowing in May.

some species (*Amaranthaceae*). A genus of half-hardy annuals with brilliant flowers of golden-yellow, and glowing shades of red, which look more like bright grasses.

Species cultivated *C. argentea*, 2 feet, tapering spikes of creamy-white flowers all summer; var. *linearis*, leaves narrower, bronze-red in autumn. *C. cristata*, the cockscomb, has tightly packed flowers in rather congested form. There are many cultivars of this, including *nana* 'Empress', 1 foot, dark foliage, crimson 'comb'; 'Golden Beauty', 1 foot, flowers dark golden yellow; *nana* 'Jewel Box', very dwarf and compact, wide colour range, orange, cream, pink, red, and bronze, new; 'Kurume Scarlet', 3 feet, foliage bright red; 'Toreador', 1½ feet, bright red, good form, can be dried and retains colour if kept away from light. *C. plumosa*, 2½ feet, Prince of Wales's Feather, the leathery species with graceful spikes of flowers; vars. 'Golden Plume'; 'Scarlet Plume'; 'Lilliput Firebrand', 1 foot. Both *C. cristata* and *C. plumosa* are sometimes looked upon as varieties of *C. argentea* and may sometimes be so listed in catalogues.

Cultivation Celosias are very good greenhouse plants. Sow seed in seed compost in a temperature of 65°F (18°C) in February. Pot up the seedlings singly, never allowing them to become potbound. Keep the atmosphere moist and plants gently growing without any check. Pot finally into 6 inch pots. Plants should be shaded throughout the summer. Bedding plants should be hardened off and planted out in the second week in June.

Centaurea (sen-taw-re-a)

From the classical myths of Greece; the plant is said to have healed a wound in the foot of Chiron, one of the Centaurs (*Compositae*). A genus of annual and perennial plants with flowers not unlike those of a thistle in structure. The annuals (cornflowers and sweet sultan) are good for cutting; some species of perennials are used as foliage plants for the silvery-white leaves.

Annual species cultivated *C. cyanus*, the cornflower, 2½ feet, a native plant, blue flower, summer. There are garden varieties in many colours, including *caerulea fl. pl.*, double blue; 'Julep', good reds. pinks and a white; 'Mauve Queen'; *nana* 'Polka Dot', 1 foot, mixed colours, good for bedding or edging, excellent range of colours including maroon; *nana* 'Rose Gem'; *rosea fl. pl.*, double pink; 'White Lady'. *C. moschata*, sweet sultan, 1½ feet, pale lilac purple, fringed petals, sweetly scented. The strain *imperialis* (Imperial Sweet Sultan), 3 feet, branching stems, mixed colours, is one of the best. Other cultivars are *alba*, white; *flava*, yellow; *rosea*, pink; 'The Bride', pure white.

Cultivation Annuals need a light friable soil with good lime content. Seed is sown in March or April where the plants are to flower and the seedlings thinned 9–12 inches apart. Tall kinds need staking. For early cut flowers, sow in August or September, keep the soil cultivated between the rows, but leave thinning until the spring.

Cheiranthus (ki-ran-thus)

Origin of name doubtful, possibly from the Arabic *kheyri*, a name for a fragrant red flower, combined with the Greek *anthos*, flower (*Cruciferae*). These are the wallflowers; there are minor botanic differences only between this genus and the genus *Erysimum*.

Species cultivated *C. allionii*, Siberian wallflower, 1 foot, bright orange, spring, hybrid, thought by some botanists to be an erysimum. *C. alpinus*, 6 inches, yellow flowers, May, Scandinavia. *C. cheiri*, the wallflower or gillyflower (note: in the eighteenth century the gillyflower was the carnation), 1–2 feet, various colours, spring, Europe, including Britain. *C.*×*kewensis*, 1 foot, sulphur yellow, orange and purple flowers, November to May, a hybrid. *C. semperflorens* (syn. *C. mutabilis*), 1 foot, purple flowers, spring, Morocco.

Cultivars Dwarf: 'Golden Bedder', 'Blood Red'; 'Orange Bedder'; 'Golden Monarch'; 'Ruby Gem'; 'Vulcan', crimson; all about 1 foot. 'Tom Thumb', mixed colours, blood red and golden-yellow; 'Harpur Crewe', golden yellow, all about 9 inches.

Early flowering: 'Yellow Phoenix'; 'Early flowering Fire King'; 'Early Flowering Vulcan'; 'Feltham Early', red and brown.

Tall and sweet-scented: 'Blood Red'; 'Scarlet Emperor'; 'Cranford Beauty', yellow; 'Eastern Queen', salmon and apricot; 'Fire King', intense flame colour; 'Primrose'; 'Cloth of Gold'; 'Ellen Willmott', ruby; 'Rose Queen'; 'Carter's White'; 'Bacchus', wine red; 'Carmine King', all 1½–2 feet.

Cultivation Wallflowers grow well in an ordinary, not too heavy, well-drained soil. The plants like chalk, so lime or old mortar may be added with advantage. Put them in sunny borders or beds or into old walls, where plants may remain perennial. Sow seed broadcast or in drills, ½ inch deep, 6 inches apart, in May. When the third leaf has formed transplant the seedlings 6 inches apart both ways in a previously limed bed of firm soil. Seedlings may be attacked by the turnip flea beetle, and it is wise to take precautionary measures by dusting the soil and the seedlings with derris or a proprietary flea beetle dust, repeating the operation at weekly intervals for several weeks. Transplant them to their final quarters in September or October at least 1 foot apart either way and make the soil firm around the roots. It is usual, though not essential, to discard plants after flowering. To grow them in walls add a little soil and well-rotted manure to holes and sow a pinch of seeds in each hole in May, or transplant young seedlings to the sites.

Wallflowers make useful early-flowering pot plants for the greenhouse. Sow seed in ordinary good soil in 6 inch pots in September, put them in a cold frame until the flower buds form and then transfer them to a greenhouse, water them moderately only and supply weak liquid manure when in flower.

Discard the plants after flowering.

Wallflowers may also be propagated by cuttings made from side shoots rooted in sandy soil. *C. alpinus*, *C. × kewensis* and *C. semperflorens* are best grown in sunny rock gardens in a mixture of loam soil and old mortar. They may be top-dressed every year with well-rotted manure.

Chrysanthemum (kris-an-the-mum)

From the Greek *chrysos*, gold, *anthemon*, flower (*Compositae*). A genus of over 100 species of annuals, herbaceous perennials and sub-shrubs, distributed over Africa, America, Asia and Europe, including Britain. The well-known greenhouse and early-flowering (outdoor) chrysanthemums are descended from *C. indicum*, found in China and Japan, and *C. morifolium* (syn. *C. sinense*), from China, two closely related, variable plants. For full details of the cultivation of these chrysanthemums see Chrysanthemum cultivation.

Annual species cultivated *C. carinatum*, 2 feet, white and yellow flowers, summer, Morocco; cultivars include *burridgeanum*, white with a crimson ring; *flore pleno hybridum*, fringed double flowers, mixed colours; 'John Bright', pure yellow; 'Lord Beaconsfield', bronze-red and bronze rings on various ground colours; 'Northern Star' white, sulphur yellow ring; 'The Sultan' coppery-scarlet; 'W. E. Gladstone', coppery-scarlet; 'White Queen'. *C. coronarium*, 1–4 feet, yellow and white, double, southern Europe; vars. 'Golden Crown', 3–4 feet, butter-yellow; 'Cream Gen', 'Golden Gem', 1 foot; 'Golden Glory', 2 feet, single. *C. frutescens*, Paris daisy, marguerite, shrubby half-hardy plant, strictly a perennial but usually treated as an annual, 2½–3 feet, white, blooming continuously, valuable greenhouse pot plant for winter, or out of doors in summer, Canary Islands; var. 'Etoile d'Or', lemon-yellow. *C. inodorum*, 9 inches, white, summer, good for cutting. *C. multicaule*, 9 inches, single golden yellow flowers, summer, Algeria. *C. nivellii*, 1 foot, white, summer, Morocco. *C. segetum*, corn marigold, yellow boy, 1½ feet, golden-yellow, summer, Europe (including Britain), Africa, Asia; vars. 'Eastern Star', yellow; 'Evening Star', golden-yellow; 'Golden Glow', double; 'Morning Star', pale yellow.

Cultivation The annuals, with the exception of *C. frutescens*, are hardy and seed is sown out of doors in April or May where the plants are to flower, in open, sunny positions and ordinary soil. An earlier start may be made by sowing under glass in spring, hardening off the seedlings and planting out in May, 6 inches apart. They may also be grown as pot plants, planting four seedlings to a 5 inch pot, seven to a 6 inch pot, growing them on in a cold frame for indoor decoration, or in the greenhouse for display purposes.

C. frutescens is propagated from cuttings taken in summer and rooted in heat in the greenhouse. The rooted cuttings are potted on, kept in a sunny place out of doors until September then moved into a cold frame until November when they are brought into the greenhouse to flower in a temperature of 50–55°F (10–13°C). Moderate watering only is required, but plants should be fed with weak liquid manure when their pots are full of roots. For outdoor cultivation in the summer cuttings are taken early in the year, grown on, hardened off and planted out in May.

1 Chrysanthemum 'Fair Lady' comes into flower in late December, a time when cultivars of this colour are not appearing freely. These plants are of moderate height with strong constitutions.
2 The 'Keystone' Chrysanthemum is a large-flowered intermediate decorative which grows to about 4 feet in height. It is especially desirable for its high resistance to weather damage.

Chrysanthemum 'Florence Shoesmith' produces a huge reflexed bloom in late autumn or early winter. It is a strong-growing cultivar of medium height.

Chrysanthemum cultivation

There are very many different kinds of chrysanthemum; however, this article is concerned only with those garden and greenhouse plants which are descended from two original species, *Chrysanthe-* *mum indicum* and *Chrysanthemum morifolium* (syn. *C. sinense*).

These hybrids may be divided into three classes according to their season of blooming. The Early-flowering type blooms in the open garden before October 1st. Mid-season varieties flower in October and November under glass and are followed in December and January by the true Late-flowering section. The glasshouse types are nor- mally grown in pots but may be planted in the open garden for the summer and lifted into the greenhouse for blooming. Flowers may, therefore, be had from August to January and there is a great variety of form and colour.

Propagation of all types is by division or cuttings, the latter giving the best results particularly for exhibition. The stools are taken up a few weeks after flowering and when the soil has been removed by washing they are boxed up in fresh compost. Since a period of dormancy is essential the boxes are kept in a cool airy place such as a cold frame and the stools kept only just moist for about a month. Slight frost will do no harm but some protection should be given when conditions are severe. Cold wet soil will cause more loss than frost.

The stronger light and higher temperatures of the spring season will cause the stools to start into growth but when cuttings have to be rooted early in the year, this process must be accelerated. A heated greenhouse is best but soil warming in the frame itself will certainly help. A temperature range of 45–55°F (7–13°C) is ideal and this must be associated with good light conditions. Once the new growth appears, watering can be increased, and the amount should be regulated according to the speed of growth. Cuttings are taken in the usual way when they are about 3 inches long. They root easily on an open bench if some muslin is stretched a few inches above them. The temperature range is as mentioned above. The time for inserting the cuttings will vary according to the facilities available and the varieties involved. Generally speaking, the early flowering-types are struck in February and March, together with those flowering in December. The mid-season varieties can be rooted from January to March.

The treatment of the young plants will vary according to the method by which they are to be grown. Plants intended for the open garden are best planted up in boxes 4 inches deep filled with potting compost or the equivalent soilless compost. Another plan is to make up a bed of compost on the floor of the cold frame. In either case, space out well at not less than 4 inches to avoid thin spindly growth. If the plants are to be flowered in large pots they should be transplanted from the cutting bed into 3 inch pots using the same compost as for boxes.

At this stage it is important to keep the plants cool and a cold frame is quite suitable in most areas from the middle of March. Plenty of light and air will keep the growth sturdy. Water the plants moderately and allow the pots and boxes to dry out between waterings. Soil kept wet all the time will encourage soft growth but overdryness produces a hard plant which can never give satisfaction. The hardening off process will aim at fully exposing the plants to

unsheltered conditions by the end of April or early May.

Plants in pots will require repotting before this time and as soon as the small pot is full of roots the plant should be moved to a 5 inch or 6 inch size, using a rich potting compost or the equivalent soilless compost. Again the emphasis should be on good spacing for maximum light while the plants should only be watered sparingly, particularly for the first few weeks. A short stake is usually needed at this time, with the stem lightly looped to it.

Plants in boxes will normally grow well until planting-out time, but if there are any signs of starvation, give a few diluted liquid feeds at weekly intervals.

During these early stages of growth the three main pests are likely to be slugs, greenfly and leafminer. The first may be controlled with metaldehyde bait, while the others succumb to sprays of BHC which should be at half the normal strength to avoid scorching tender foliage.

From early May the treatment of plants varies according to type and it is necessary to follow each method separately.

Early-flowering chrysanthemums These are flowered in the open garden and the ground must be well prepared during the winter. The main aims are to provide

After lifting, the chrysanthemum stools are 1) washed free of soil and 2) the basal shoots cut away. Plant the stools in clean boxes as close together as is convenient. 3) Special attention needs to be paid to labelling. 4) To avoid confusion, keep one variety in each box, but if this is not possible, label each stool separately. 5) Use soil which has not previously been used as the rooting medium for chrysanthemums. 6) Water the stools in and stand in a light cool place. A cold frame is ideal. Growth will start when the temperature is raised to 45–50° F (7–13° C).

plenty of humus for moisture retention and sufficient nourishment to sustain the plants in full growth for a period of several months. The basic method is to dig the land one spit deep incorporating farmyard manure or compost at the rate of one bucket per square yard. At the same time, dust the trenches with bonemeal, using $\frac{1}{2}$–$\frac{3}{4}$ lb per square yard. The ground is left rough for weathering until the middle of April when a light forking over is given. This should never go deeper than 3–4 inches but this surface layer must be enriched by working in a base fertilizer or a similar general fertilizer at $\frac{1}{4}$ lb per square yard. This programme provides nourishment immediately available at the surface for the young roots and slow acting organic

material at lower levels to serve the mature plant. Lime is required only if the soil is rather acid (pH less than 6·5). Where plants are to be grown in rows on a separate plot, this cultivation should be given to the whole area but if plants are to form groups in a border the same kind of preparation may be given to the actual planting sites.

A careful raking will level the soil and prepare a good planting tilth in early May and the actual moving of the plants may be done from about May 10th in the south if the weather is suitable. The first step is to place the canes either in rows or groups according to the site. Plants should never be closer than 18 inches and rows can be double, leaving paths 2½ feet wide between each pair. Planting may be done when the soil is nicely moist without being sticky. A hole is taken out close to the cane and large enough to contain the root ball without cramping. If soil preparation was not well done or the soil tends to be poor, it is a good idea to incorporate a handful of peat and a sprinkling of base fertilizer in the bottom of the hole. Water the boxes some hours beforehand so that the plants may be removed from them with little damage to the roots. Plant firmly at the same level and immediately give one loose tie around the cane to avoid breakages. It is better not to water in but if the weather is dry try to keep the plants going with overhead sprays of water until a shower comes. When watering is essential give a substantial amount so as to wet the soil quite deeply.

Slugs may still be troublesome and appropriate action must be taken. In built-up areas birds may become a problem, as they peck at leaves and growing points with unfortunate results. Black cotton string stretched in criss-cross fashion a few inches above the tips still seems to be the best answer. The birds stop attacking the plants after a few weeks and the string can be removed to make hoeing easier.

It is important to keep the plants growing steadily without any check and in dry weather a thorough watering may be necessary every week though a mulch of compost, peat or lawn mowings may help on light soils. Feeding will also help, but it should not be overdone. One application of fertilizer at the end of May and another at the end of June should be quite enough if the winter cultivation was well done. Each time use a fertilizer containing about twice the amount of nitrogen as potash. Throughout the growing season keep the ground free of weeds but resort to hand weeding after mid-June to avoid damaging the surface roots. Pests will cause trouble, and particular attention should be given in July and August when capsid bugs are active. A fungicidal spray every ten days should prevent significant damage. Tying-in of the stems is also very important. They may either be looped to a strong central cane or enclosed in a framework of three canes. In either case allow some movement of the stems, for in this way they will bend before the wind. Too rigid a support often results in breakage.

The pinching and disbudding process for large blooms follows the same pattern for early-flowering and late-flowering and will be described fully in a later paragraph.

Late-flowering chrysanthemums These plants are grown on in the 5–6 inch pots for several weeks but before they become pot bound they must be potted on to their final sizes. The 9 inch size is the most useful pot but both 8 inch and 10 inch may be used. For the very best results the following crop may be taken:

Large exhibition blooms Two blooms in a 10 inch pot or one only to an 8 inch.

Incurveds and decoratives Three blooms in an 8 inch pot or four to a 9 inch. The 10 inch size is only used for the very vigorous plants when up to six blooms may be taken.

Singles Best quality is obtained when four blooms are taken from an 8 inch and two more for every inch increase in the size of pot.

These figures are for blooms of exhibition quality but for good cut-flowers one may safely increase the crop by 50 per cent in each instance.

The final potting which is usually necessary in early June, must be done carefully. Potting compost is advised, or the equivalent soilless compost. The first step is to provide adequate drainage in the bottom of the pot, covering the bottom layer of large crocks with smaller ones and placing on top of this a thin layer of peat or the coarser material of the compost. Place the root ball on the coarse material and add compost until the final level is some 3 inches below the rim. New compost is added and some gentle firming must be done as each handful is placed. Modern practice does not favour the heavy ramming which was once the custom. When peat/sand composts are used, no firming of any kind is necessary.

If the plants were watered several hours before potting, there will be no need to water them in, indeed it is best to place the newly-potted stock in a cool, shady place and provide them with overhead sprays of water as long as possible. Under good conditions it may not be necessary to water for between four to seven days. When water is obviously needed give sufficient to fill the whole 3 inches of free space which has been left at the top of the pot. Thereafter, each plant should be watered according to its needs, allowing the soil to dry out almost to the point of causing the plant to flag a little before watering again. It is difficult to describe the precise state the soil should have reached, but the grower will soon become expert at judging the correct time to water.

Once the plants are established in their new pots they may be stood out in rows for the summer. The standing ground should be in full sun and the rows of plants set out with wide paths for easy access. The maximum room available should be given to each plant and it is best to stand the pots on slates, planks or gravel to discourage the entry of worms and to ensure free drainage of surplus water. The canes inserted at final potting must be securely tied to a straining wire stretched about $3\frac{1}{2}$ feet above the pots. If these wires are supported by firm end posts, there will be no fear of damage by winds which always

1 Cuttings of chrysanthemums are made from strong sturdy shoots taken from the base of the plant, 2 to 3 inches in length.
2 The lower leaves are removed and the cutting inserted firmly, about an inch deep, with a wooden dibber into a special compost covered with sand.
3 Each container should be clearly labelled with the variety name and the cuttings then watered in.
4 Stand the pots close together in a cool, shaded greenhouse or frame until rooting occurs.

seem to come in September when the plants are large.

Pest control, tying and watering will all need attention through the growing season but a major concern will be feeding, since the roots, being confined to a limited volume of soil, will need extra help to produce fine plants. Much could be written on this subject but a basic programme involves the application of dry fertilizer once weekly at the rate of one teaspoonful per pot or at such rates as the manufacturer may specify. This begins about the first week in July and the fertilizer should be of a fairly high nitrogen content to encourage the growth of leaf and stem. Later on when the bud arrives, the fertilizer is changed to one which has about equal quantities of nitrogen and potash. Liquid fertilizers are probably better and here one may give a feed every two days using a quarter-strength dilution. All feeding should stop when the plants are taken inside to flower.

This process of housing takes place

Individual blooms can be protected from damage and pollution with paper bags secured with waterproof glue. Two, one inside the other, are used. Inflate by blowing into them and place over buds which are opening.

about the end of September and is preceded by a thorough cleaning of the house followed by a fumigation with BHC or a sulphur candle to rid it of all pests. The plants themselves require preparation, and this involves the removal of the old leaves at the base and a spraying of all foliage with a combination of insecticide and fungicide. A good combination would be dinocap and BHC. It is important to wet the undersides of the foliage where many mildew troubles begin.

Once the plants are dry, they may be taken inside and arranged in convenient rows, giving them as much space as possible to allow light and air to flow around the lower leaves. For the first fortnight, every ventilator and door can

be left open by day and night but as the buds begin to open it will be necessary to regulate ventilation in conjunction with gentle heat to keep the air dry and moving and at a temperature of 50–55°F (10–13°C). Shading on the roof is an added refinement to prevent scorching from very bright morning sunshine. Indoors the plants may not require so much watering but it should be done carefully and early in the day, so that the air is dry before closing some of the ventilators at night. There must always be some ventilators left open except in very foggy conditions and even then it is better to have a little ventilation with enough heat to exclude the moisture. Pests may be controlled by the use of an aerosol or by routine fumigations.

Stopping If left to grow naturally the chrysanthemum plant will extend its single stem until a bud forms at the tip. This is the break bud which causes the plant to break into branching growth. Usually the grower will pinch out the tip of his plant before this bud forms

1

2

3

4

5

6

and this process is sometimes called 'stopping'. It has the same result in the formation of lateral branches and is a useful device to help in timing flowers for a particular date. Each of the side branches ultimately forms a bud at its tip. This is the first crown bud and is usually the one which is 'taken' or allowed to flower. In the few instances—such as the singles—where the second crown is the desired bud, the plant may be pinched or stopped a second time, thus producing further laterals and increasing the potential flower crop. Most chrysanthemum catalogues give the best dates on which to pinch each variety to obtain blooms at the normal show season, but the gardener who is growing for cut-flowers may ignore these dates and follow the following alternative plan.

Early flowering: Pinch the plants when they are about 6–9 inches high and take on four to six stems. For decorative plants in the border, double this number of stems may be kept. For exhibition

Early-flowering chrysanthemums are brought into flower in the open garden, in soil deeply dug in winter. In April prepare a tilth by forking 3 to 4 inches deep and applying a general fertilizer at 4 oz per square yard. In mid-May the plants are stood out in rows at least 18 inches apart. 1) At the time of planting, a hole is dug large enough to take the root ball without overcrowding. 2) The plant is knocked out of its pot. Water first to prevent damage to the roots. 3) Remove crocks and pebbles and 4) plant. 5) and 6) Firm the soil. If the ground is dry, water in the plants. They will also require staking at a later date.

quality three only are retained.

Mid season: Pinch when plants are about 9 inches high and allow the required number of stems to grow on. If the number produced is not sufficient, pinch again and allow the requisite number to extend to bud.

Late flowering: Pinch for the first time at 9 inches high and give a further

pinch at the end of July.

Disbudding If left to develop naturally, the chrysanthemum will flower in sprays but if it is desired to produce large specimen blooms the buds must be restricted to one per stem. Unless it has been damaged, the central or crown bud is retained and all the buds or sideshoots clustered around it removed. The removal should begin when the sideshoots are about $\frac{1}{2}$ inch long and it is advisable to take out one each day over a period. The sideshoots which are produced lower down the plant, together with the suckers appearing from the soil, may be removed as soon as they are seen so that all the energies of the plant are directed to the flowering stems.

Timing Production of blooms for a specific date is not the easiest task, since it is controlled by many factors. The dates on which the plants are rooted and pinched will have some bearing and the optimum dates for each variety can usually be ascertained from catalogues and other publications.

The buds of early-flowering types to give bloom in the first half of September should arrive from mid-July to the first week of August. The mid-seasons normally bloom in the first two weeks of November and buds should appear at the following times according to type:

Large Exhibition   August 10-20th
Incurveds and Decoratives

     end of August
Singles   around September 7-14th

There is little one can do to hurry a bud which is late but early buds can be dealt with in one of three ways. If the bud is more than three weeks earlier than desired, it is best to pinch each stem and allow the next crown bud to form. Buds only two or three weeks early may be 'run on.' This means that the bud is removed together with all the side shoots around it except for the topmost one. This is allowed to grow on as an extension of the main stem to form another bud in a few weeks. Buds which are only a few days early may be delayed somewhat by leaving the sideshoots around the bud to grow to an inch or so before disbudding begins.

Protecting blooms In exposed gardens or in areas of polluted air it may be necessary to protect the choicer outdoor blooms from damage. Light wooden frames covered with polythene may be firmly fixed over the beds. Another method widely used by exhibitors consists of enclosing individual blooms within paper bags specially made with waterproof glue. Two bags, one within the other are used, and after being inflated with the breath they are placed over the opening bud which has previously been sprayed and allowed to dry. The mouth of the bag is gathered up to the stem and secured firmly with two green twist ties about 2 inches apart. No protection of any kind should be placed on the buds until the stem immediately below is firm and strong and the first colour is seen in the florets. White and yellow blooms bag well but other colours tend to fade badly.

Soilless composts It is not always possible to rely on the quality of composts bought from the shops and the supply of good quality loam for home mixing is very limited. For these reasons it may be profitable to use soilless composts for all pot work. Experience suggests that these composts will satisfy most requirements, but the grower must be ready to follow the instructions quite closely. These composts are not recommended for boxing up the early-flowering plants, for the root action is so vigorous that it is almost impossible to separate the plants at planting-out time without causing very serious damage to the roots.

Recommended cultivars Because of the large number of cultivars available and the steady stream of novelties each year, the following list can only indicate some of the best varieties at the present time. They are set out according to the National Chrysanthemum Society of Great Britain's classification.

Indoor varieties: Section 1 Large Exhibition 'Duke of Kent' white, 3½ feet, reflexed, stop May 15th for first crown; 'Yellow Duke' is also very fine and treatment is the same. 'Gigantic', salmon, 4½ feet, reflexed, stop May 7th for first crown. 'Majestic', light bronze, 3 feet, reflexed, stop May 7th for first crown; 'Yellow Majestic' and 'Red Majestic' are equally as good and should be treated in the same way, 'Shirley Primrose', yellow, 5-6 feet, interlacing florets. Root in January and allow the plants to break twice to give second crown buds.

Section 2 Medium Exhibition 'Cosack', red, 4 feet, very reliable. Root in January and February and stop at mid-June for first crown. 'Connie Mayhew', yellow, 5 feet, deep primrose incurved bloom. Let

1 Chrysanthemums with quilled petals are popular in flower arrangements.
2 Anemone-flowered chrysanthemums flower on second crown buds.

plants form their break naturally and take the first crown.

Section 3 Exhibition Incurveds: *Large-flowered* 'Audrey Shoesmith', pink, 5 feet, strong healthy grower, blooms are very tight. Stop on June 1st for first crown. There is a 'White Audrey Shoesmith' which responds to the same treatment. 'Lilian Shoesmith' is a bronze. The plants are dwarfer at 4 feet and should be pinched at mid-June. 'Shirley Model' is of recent introduction. The rich pink blooms are borne on upright plants of about 4 feet. Stop third week of May.

Medium-flowered 'Maylen', white, 4 feet, is the parent of a large family including yellow, golden and buff coloured sports. All give good blooms if stopped twice, June 1st and July 7th for second crowns. 'Vera Woolman', yellow, is similar in height and stopping requirements. 'Minstrel Boy', light bronze, is possibly the best in this section. Reaching 4½ feet, this one also needs two stops, June 1st and June 30th.

Section 4 Reflexed Decoratives: *Large-flowered* There is a shortage of good cultivars in this section. 'Stuart Shoesmith' light bronze, 4½ feet, is a very easy grower. Stop June 15th for first crown. 'Elizabeth Woolman' pink, and the salmon sport reach only 3 feet, and should be allowed to make a natural break or be stopped in late June.

Medium-flowered 'Joy Hughes', pink, 4½ feet, deeply reflexing spiky florets. Root in February and allow to make a natural break for first crown. Often needs frequent watering. 'Princess Anne', pink, 3½ feet. Its only fault is a spreading habit which calls for careful

tying-up. There are several sports including 'Yellow Princess Anne' which is probably the best of the family. The whole family produces its best flowers on second crown buds after the plants have been stopped on June 1st and July 7th. 'Woking Scarlet', red, 3½ feet, an excellent cut flower when stopped about mid-June allowing the first crown bud to form and then rubbing it out to run-on for second crown.

Section 5 Intermediate Decoratives These are neither incurved nor fully reflexing. *Large-flowered* 'Balcombe Perfection', bronze, 3½ feet, parent of a family including red, and golden sports. For November flowering stop once only on June 1st. For December a second stop may be given at the end of July. 'Fair Lady', pink, 3½ feet, a most beautiful incurving form in carnation pink, with very neat habit. Stop June 15th for first crown. The bronze and orange sports are also highly desirable. 'Goldfoil', yellow, 3½ feet, clear yellow and very resistant to damping. Stop end of June. 'Daily Mirror', purple, 4½ feet, a recent introduction of great worth though not everyone's choice of colour. Stop twice, June 1st and 30th.

Medium-flowered 'Leslie Tandy', purple, 4 feet, very full blooms with a touch of silver. There is also a red sport. Stop June 7th for first crown. 'Woking Perfection', red, 4½ feet, hard, long-lasting blooms. Best rooted in February and stopped once only in mid-June.

Section 7 Singles: *Large-flowered* 'Albert Cooper', yellow, 4½ feet: 'Broadacre', white, 3½ feet; 'Preference', pink, 4½ feet; 'Woolman's Glory', bronze, 4½ feet; 'Red Woolman's Glory', red, 4½ feet. All should be stopped twice, mid-May and late-June.

Medium-flowered 'Golden Seal', yellow, 3 feet; 'Mason's Bronze', bronze, 5 feet, and several colours sports including 'Chesswood Beauty', red 'Jinx', white, 4 feet. Stopping times are as for the large-flowered.

Decoratives for December and Christmas 'Christmas Wine', pink; 'Bellona', pink; the Favourite family including white, golden, pink and red; 'Fred Shoesmith', and its sports; 'Loula', red. These should all be stopped twice, the first time when they are about 9 inches high and again at the end of July. 'Mayford Perfection', and its many sports are also very good but these must be grown on natural first crowns.

The so-called American Sprays are useful for the November–December period and there is a variety of form ranging from singles to pompons. It is

1 Chrysanthemum 'Pretty Polly' is a medium-flowered reflexed decorative.
2 Cascade chrysanthemums, widely used in Victorian conservatories, are still popular for decoration. Flowering occurs over a period of six months.

best to obtain young plants in June, for early rooting leads to excessive height. Stop once only when they are about 9 inches high and then leave them to branch naturally. No disbudding is practised and the flowers come in dainty sprays. 'American Snow', white; 'Christmas Greeting', red; 'Corsair', yellow; 'Galaxy', bronze; 'Minstrel', pink, can all be recommended.

Outdoor cultivars All are flowered on first crown buds.

Section 23 Incurved Decoratives: *Large-flowered* 'Ermine', white, 4½ feet, stands alone in this section. Thin stems but strong and healthy. There is a yellow sport of less quality. Stop June 7th. Bags well.

Medium-flowered 'Martin Riley', yellow, 4 feet, long-lasting blooms tending to come in August. Stop at mid-June. 'Yellow Nugget', yellow, 3½ feet, excellent flowers on a sturdy plant, bags well.

Section 24 Reflexed Decoratives: *Large-flowered* 'Ken Cooper', yellow, 3½ feet, of immaculate form and clear colour. Stop June 15th. 'Polaris', white, 3 feet, a quality flower with long, plunging florets, stop June 1st. 'Standard', bronze, 4 feet. Bright orange-bronze and top of its class, stop May 20th. 'Tracy Waller', pink with salmon, bronze and cherry sports, all at 5 feet. The height makes these a little difficult but the flowers are superb. Stop on June 1st.

Medium-flowered 'Early Red Cloak', red, 3½ feet, strong prolific grower. Flowers of fine form and the colour fades but little. Stop June 7th. 'Morley Jones', 3 feet, colour is rich amber with peach suffusion. Perfectly weather-proof and suitable for exhibition or bedding. Stop June 15th. 'Pretty Polly', purple, 2½ feet. Good for all purposes, the flowers being weatherproof. Stop June 1st. 'Sonny Riley', yellow, 4 feet, possibly the best in this section with high quality flowers. Bags well and always blooms well. Stop June 1st.

Section 25 Intermediate Decoratives: *Large-flowered* 'Evelyn Bush', white, 4½ feet, mainly an exhibitor's flower as it comes best out of bags. Stop June 1st. 'Gladys Sharpe', yellow, 3 feet, very strong grower with large foliage and full blooms. Stop mid-May. 'Harry James', bronze, 4 feet, reddish bronze florets which are broad and closely incurving. Blooms late in September, so stop mid-May. 'Keystone', purple, and its sport 'Red Keystone' reach about 4 feet. Highly resistant to weather damage Stop in early June.

Medium-flowered 'Cricket', white, with yellow and primrose sports, 4 feet, blooms last well after cutting. Stop June 7th. 'Jane Rowe', pale pink, 3½ feet, new but very promising though the delicate colour fades in bright sunshine. Stop June 15th. 'People', purple, 4½ feet, of exquisite form showing the reverse of the florets. Tends to bloom in the second half of September so stop mid-May.

Cineraria hybrida grandiflora is typical of modern strains.

'Topper', light bronze, 3½ feet, a lovely flower which bags well with little loss of colour. Stop June 1st.

Outdoor Singles are not very distinguished but 'Kitty' may be tried, while 'Premiere', an anemone-centred type, is also worth a place.

Any of the Pompons are good and they are available in varying heights and colour. Give one pinch when the plants are established outside, and then leave them to develop naturally.

A selection for bedding In addition to the shorter cultivars among those already listed, the following are recommended: August-flowering. 'Sweetheart', pink, and its many sports, 3 feet; 'Capstan', bronze, 2½ feet; 'Sunavon', yellow, 3 feet; 'Red flare', red, 3 feet.
September-flowering. 'Whiteball', white,

2½ feet; 'Catherine Porter', pink, 3 feet; 'Packwell', bronze, 3½ feet; 'J. R. Johnson', yellow, 3½ feet.

All these should be stopped about June 7th. They may be allowed to flower in sprays or be disbudded for larger blooms.

Cineraria (sin-er-air-e-a)
From the Latin *cinereus*, ash-coloured, referring to the colour of the undersides of the leaves. All but a very few species (none of which are likely to be found in cultivation) have been transferred to the genus *Senecio* and for information on cinerarias other than the florist's cinerarias, see Senecio.

Florist's cinerarias The florist's cinerarias, obtainable in a very wide range of beautiful colours, have been derived from *Senecio cruentus* (once known as *Cineraria cruenta*), a herbaceous perennial from the Canary Islands. Although

the plants are strictly perennials they are almost invariably grown as half-hardy annuals or biennials, for greenhouse display or for spring window boxes. Seed is obtainable of various strains in mixed colours, under such names as *hybrida grandiflora*, producing plants about 18–24 inches tall; 'Berlin Market', not quite so tall, in various rich shades; 'Hansa Strain', 18 inches, bright colours, compact plants; 'Rainbow', 18 inches, pinks and pale blues; 'Cremer's Prize', 18 inches, medium-sized flowers, freely produced; *stellata*, 2½ feet, large heads of small, star-shaped flowers in very varied colours; *multiflora nana*, 1 foot, dwarf plants, self-coloured flowers. In addition there are certain named colour cultivars growing to about 21 inches tall, including *atroviolacea*, large dark violet flowers; 'Matador', coppery scarlet; *sanguinea*, blood-red.

Cultivation To produce winter-flowering plants seed should be sown in April or early May in the heated greenhouse, in a temperature of 55–60°F (13–16°C). Seed for spring-flowering plants should be sown in an unheated frame in June or early July. Sow thinly in seed compost, covering the seed only lightly. When the seedlings have developed three leaves pot them up into deep seed boxes. Give

Cinerarias are colourful and deservedly popular as house plants, but they are suitable as well for window boxes and summer bedding. They need a cool airy position with full light.

them plenty of light and air; pot them on again singly into 3 inch pots before they become crowded, then into 6 inch pots when the 3 inch pots are filled with roots. Large, vigorous plants may need a further potting into 7 or 8 inch pots; this should be done by the end of October. Potting composts are perfectly suitable. Once they have been potted singly the plants should be moved out into the cold frame and kept shaded. They may remain there until about mid-October, given plenty of ventilation, both by day and by night. They will still need ample ventilation after they have been brought into the greenhouse where they should be placed on the staging as near to the glass as possible. Feed the plants with weak liquid manure or fertilizer, twice weekly from September onwards and spray them against attacks by aphids and leaf miners. From late October until the plants have finished flowering and are either discarded or used to provide cuttings, the temperature in the greenhouse should be 45–50°F (7–10°C). How

ever, cuttings are hardly ever used to propagate these plants, unless it is to increase a specially desirable variety.

Cladanthus (klad-an-thus)
From the Greek *klados*, branch, *anthos*, flower, referring to the flowers borne at the ends of the branched shoots (*Compositae*). A genus of a single species, a half-hardy annual with yellow-rayed flowers carried at the ends of the branches. The species is *C. arabicus* (syns. *C. proliferus*, *Anthemis arabica*), 2½–3 feet, a strong smelling plant, a native of Spain and Morocco.
Cultivation Seed should be sown in the greenhouse in spring and the plants set out in their flowering quarters in late May. The plants will grow in any ordinary garden soil.

Clarkia (klar-ke-a)
Commerating Captain William Clark, who with Captain Meriwether Lewis made a famous journey through America and across the Rocky Mountains early in the nineteenth century (*Onagraceae*). A small genus of hardy annuals from North America, of which one species only, the popular *C. elegans*, is likely to be encountered in general cultivation. Of this, however, there are

many fine cultivars in a good colour range.

They include 'Brilliant', double carmine; 'Enchantress', double salmon-pink; 'Fire-brand', scarlet; 'Glorious', bright crimson, dark leaves; 'Illumination', orange and rose-pink; 'Lady Satin Rose', double; 'May Blossom', double pink; 'Orange King'; 'Purple King', double; 'Salmon Bouquet'. All these grow to about 2 feet tall. There are also mixed strains available as well as the 'Royal Bouquet' mixed strain, slightly dwarfer.

Cultivation Clarkias do best in a light rich soil in a sunny border or bed. Space the plants well apart to obtain the best results. Propagate from seed sown ⅛ inch deep in April, May or June in rows or clumps where the plants are required to flower, as they do not transplant well. Thin the seedlings to 8 inches apart when they are 3 inches high. Clarkias may also be grown as greenhouse plants. Sow seeds in small pots of loamy soil in September and grow the plants on in cool, airy conditions until spring, when they should be re-potted into loamy soil for flowering. The stems, whether grown in pots or out of doors, may need a few twigs among them for support.

Cleome (kle-o-me)

The old Greek name (*Capparadiceae*). A genus, mainly of half-hardy or green-house annuals of which the best known is *C. spinosa*, the spider flower, a striking half-hardy annual with spidery flowers which can be grown outside in summer.

Species cultivated *C. hirta*, 4 feet, bluish-green foliage, pinkish-mauve flowers, summer. *C. lutea*, 1 foot, yellow-orange flowers, July and August. *C. spinosa*, spider flower, 3–4 feet, white, pale pink or rose-pink flowers, June to September; cultivars include: 'Helen Campbell', white; 'Mauve Queen'; 'Pink Queen'; 'Rose Queen'; all colours as indicated by their names.

Cultivation Sow seed ¹⁄₁₆ inch deep in a temperature of 65–70°F (18 21°C) in March, potting the seedlings into individual pots when they are 1 inch tall. If they are to be grown out of doors, grow them on steadily, potting on as required, harden off in May for planting out in a light, rich soil in a sunny dry spot in early June. They make fine greenhouse pot plants, grown in potting compost. Water only moderately at all times.

Cobaea (ko-be-a)

Commerating Father Barnadez Cobo, a Spanish Jesuit and naturalist, who

1 Cladanthus arabicus is a half-hardy annual with a strong pungent odour.
2 Clarkia, a genus of four or five species from North America, has many colour forms.

lived in Mexico, the home of these plants (*Polemoniaceae*). A small genus of tender perennial plants, climbing by means of tendrils, usually grown as annuals. One species only is likely to be found in cultivation. This is *C. scandens*, the cup-and-saucer vine, so named because of the shape of the beautiful long-stemmed flowers, which resemble those of a Canterbury bell. They open cream and gradually turn deep purple. They appear continuously from May to October, or even throughout the winter. A quick-growing evergreen climber to 20 feet, this is particularly useful for large conservatories where two or three plants can soon cover a wall. There is a white-flowered form, *flore albo*, and a variegated form, *variegata*.

Cultivation Seed should be sown (edgeways in the pots) in a temperature of 50–55°F (10–13°C) in late February, or in a frame in April and young plants potted up singly when they have made two or three leaves. They can then either be planted out-of-doors in June in sheltered gardens or planted in a cold greenhouse or conservatory border. Alternatively, they can be potted in large pots or tubs in a compost of equal parts of leafmould and loam with a scattering of sand, and the laterals pinched back to two or three buds to prevent straggly growth. Water regularly and feed weekly with a liquid feed during the early summer.

Plants occasionally survive the winter out of doors in the south but are usually so slow to make new growth that much quicker results are obtained by raising new plants from seed. They may be grown in a light, warm living room, but need ample space and adequate support for their tendrils. A sticky nectar is liable to drop from the open flowers, so the position indoors should be chosen with some care.

Collinsia (kol-in-ze-a)
Commerating Zaccheus Collins, American naturalist (*Scrophulariaceae*). Hardy annuals from North America and Mexico, related to *Penstemon*, easy to grow and bearing spikes of attractive blossom during summer. The only species likely to be found in cultivation is *C. bicolor*, 12–15 inches, with lilac and white flowers. It has several varieties including *alba*, white; *multicolor*, rose, lilac and white; 'Salmon Beauty', salmon rose. Seed of mixed varieties is also available.

Cultivation Collinsias like sunny borders,

1 Cleome spinosa, the Spider Flower, is an annual discovered in the West Indies. It thrives outside in summer or as a greenhouse pot plant in cold weather. 2 Cobaea scandens, a half-hardy climber from South America, is best grown in a pot or tub that can be moved indoors for the winter months.

and look especially effective among mixed annuals. They do well in ordinary soil. Propagation is by seed sown out of doors during the spring, where plants are intended to flower. It pays to sow thinly. Final thinning should take place when young plants are 2 inches high; allow 6 inches between each. Collinsias may also be sown out of doors in a sheltered spot during September and allowed to stand throughout the winter for flowering during June.

Convolvulus (kon-vol-vu-lus)

From the Latin *convolvo*, to entwine, as some of the species do (*Convolvulaceae*). A valuable race of plants both annual and perennial, herbaceous or sub-shrubby. Flowers are bell-shaped throughout and highly attractive.

Hardy annual species cultivated *C. tricolor* (syn. *C. minor*), 1 foot, blue, pink and white flowers, late summer; cultivars include 'Cambridge Blue'; 'Crimson Monarch', cherry red with white and gold centre; 'Lavender Rosette'; 'Royal Ensign', Wedgwood blue with gold centre; 'Royal Marine', rich blue. For *C. major* see *Ipomoea purpurea*.

Cultivation These convolvulus can be grown in beds and borders and appreciate good soil and sun. Trailing species may be provided with support if preferred. A sunny, sheltered rock garden is especially suitable for *C. cneorum*, *C. mauritanicus* and other dwarf and trailing species. Propagation of hardier kinds is by seed sown out of doors in spring. Strike cuttings of *C. cneorum* and *C. mauritanicus* in sandy soil in a frame in July and August. Bottom heat is an advantage.

Coreopsis (kor-e-op-sis)

From the Greek *koris*, a bug or tick, *opsis*, like, a reference to the appearance of the seeds (*Compositae*). Tickseed. The annual species are often catalogued under *Calliopsis*. Hardy perennials and annuals with showy flowers, excellent for borders.

Annual species cultivated *C. atkinsoniana*, 2–4 feet, yellow and purple flowers, summer. *C. basalis* (syn. *C. cardaminifolia*), 6 inches–2 feet, yellow and purplish flowers, summer. *C. coronata*, 2 feet, orange and crimson flowers, summer. *C. drummondii*, 2 feet, yellow and crimson flowers, summer: a cultivar is 'Golden Crown'. *C. tinctoria* (syn. *C. bicolor*), 2 feet, yellow and crimson

1 Collinsia bicolor, a hardy annual growing to 2 feet, flowers in late summer. First discovered in California, Collinsias resemble, and are closely-related to, Penstemons, but there are minor botanical differences. Seed can be sown either in spring or in autumn.

2 Convolvulus cneorum is a half-hardy sub-shrub from southern Europe which requires a cold greenhouse in cooler areas.

flowers, summer; cultivars include 'Crimson King', 9 inches; 'Fire King' 9 inches, scarlet; 'Golden Sovereign', 9 inches; 'Dazzler', 9 inches, crimson and yellow; 'Star of Fire', 9–12 inches, red; 'Evening Star', 9 inches, yellow and scarlet; 'The Garnet', 1½ feet crimson-scarlet; 'Tiger Star', 12 inches, bronze and yellow; 'Golden Blaze', 2–3 feet, gold and maroon, yellow and maroon; 'Sovereign', 9 inches, golden-yellow.

Cultivation Coreopsis do well in ordinary well-drained garden soil and in sunny positions. Plant perennials during autumn and spring. Propagate single perennial species from cuttings in April, or seed sown a month later; double forms by cuttings in April. Split large clumps in autumn. The annuals are raised from seed sown out of doors during spring and early summer, where they are intended to flower, thinning the seedlings to 9 inches. Alternatively, seed may be sown under glass in a temperature of 65°F (18°C) in March.

Cosmos (koz-mos)
From the Greek *kosmos*, beautiful (*Compositae*). Half-hardy annuals and perennials, mainly from tropical America, with ferny foliage and broad-petalled, daisy flowers, single and sometimes double. They are sometimes found in catalogues under the name *Cosmea*.
Species cultivated *C. atrosanguineus*, 1–3 feet, dark brownish-red flowers, late summer to early autumn, perennial, treated as an annual. *C. bipinnatus*, 3 feet, rose or purple, late summer. *C. diversifolius* (syn. *Bidens dahlioides*), 3 feet, lilac flowers, late summer to early autumn. *C. sulphureus*, 3–4 feet, pale yellow flowers, mid to late summer. Cultivars and strains in many hues are numerous. Those of *C. bipinnatus* include 'Early Flowering Crimson-Scarlet',

'Fairy Queen', bright rose; 'Sensation' pink and white; 'Sensation Purity' white; 'Sensation Radiance', rose and crimson bicolor; 'Crested Mixed', double in varied colours. Cultivars of *C. sulphureus* are 'Klondyke Orange Flare' and 'Klondyke Yellow Flare'.
Cultivation Cosmos will grow in almost any good garden soil, especially the lighter kinds and should be given a sunny position. Propagation is by seed sown in a temperature of 55–60°F (13–16°C) from February to March. Prick out the seedlings into boxes in which they are grown on and finally hardened off. Plant out at the end of May, 1 foot apart. Plants will become large and in high summer are loaded with flowers which are ideal for cutting.

Delphinium (del-fin-e-um)
From the Greek *delphin*, a dolphin, the flowerbuds having some resemblance to that sea creature (*Ranunculaceae*). Larkspur. The genus consists of annual, biennial and herbaceous perennial plants, mostly hardy and showy plants for border cultivation, with some dwarf species suitable for the rock garden.
Species cultivated: Annual *D. ajacis*, 1–2 feet, blue, violet, rose-pink or white, summer, Europe, *D. consolida*, branching larkspur, 2 feet, purple or deep violet, summer, Europe. *D. paniculatum*, Siberian larkspur, up to 3 feet, single, violet, July to September, also grown as a biennial. Seedsmen list many beautiful varieties of these annual larkspurs, mainly 2½–3 feet tall, derived mainly from *D. ajacis* and *D. consolida*. They

1 Cultivars of Coreopsis, the Tickseed, are easy to raise from seed.
2 and 3 Cosmos bipinnatus, a Mexican annual, reaches 3 feet in height and flowers in late summer.

include such strains as 'Giant Hyacinth flowered'; 'Giant Imperial'; 'Regal', 4 feet; 'Supreme', 4 feet, and named cultivars such as 'Blue Spire', dark blue; 'Carmine King'; 'Dazzler', bright scarlet; 'Exquisite Pink'; 'Lilac Spire'; 'Los Angeles', rose and salmon; 'Miss California', salmon rose; 'Rosamond', bright rose and 'White Spire'.
Cultivation Sow annual varieties in a sunny, open border in April where they are to flower, or in boxes of light soil under glass in March in a temperature of 55°F (13°C). Prick out seedlings when large enough to handle and transplant in the open in May.
Cultivation of modern hybrid delphiniums Fast growing plants, delphiniums require a deeply-dug, rich soil with adequate drainage. A medium loam is preferable to a light sandy soil. Where the soil is light, dig in deeply plenty of compost or old farmyard manure before planting and during the summer a mulch of garden compost is excellent. Nitrogenous fertilizers should be used with care as they may only result in producing weak stems. If the stems are cut back immediately after flowering a second crop of spikes may be produced,

1

2

3

4

1 This border of Delphiniums in various shades of purple is in Regent's Park, London.
2, 3 and 4 Delphiniums are available in a wide range of colour and bloom type.

but these should only be encouraged with strong-growing varieties. Adequate moisture will be required to produce this second crop during what may be hot, summer weather. Slugs can be a menace with the tender young delphinium shoots, especially in the early spring, so precautions should be taken with slug pellets or other repellents. Varieties that grow to about 4–5 feet in height are more suitable for small gardens than those that tower to 7 feet or more, and they are less liable to damage by summer gales. Pea sticks, brushwood or twigs can be used to support the young growths but these should be put in position around the plants in good time so that the stems grow up through them. This is often left too late, with the result that the tender stems get broken when the sticks are being pushed into the soil. Staking for exhibition spikes must be carefully done, using one stout cane to each spike. When growing the large flowering varieties it is usual to restrict one-year-old plants to one spike and two-year-old plants to two or three spikes. Pea sticks, however, provide adequate support for the lighter, less tall graceful belladonna types of delphinium, with their branching stems, which are also so attractive for floral arrangement. Exhibition spikes should be straight, tapering and well-filled with large circular florets (but not overcrowded) and bearing few laterals. The foliage should be clean, healthy and undamaged. As soon as spikes are cut they should be placed in deep containers filled with water and stood in a cool, but not draughty, place. There they should remain for some hours or overnight. Each stem should be wrapped in a large sheet of tissue paper (30 × 40 inches) before being taken to the show. A further step to ensure that the spike does not flag is to turn it upside down, immediately before final staging, fill the hollow stem with cold water and plug with cotton wool.

As it is easily raised from seed, the delphinium has been of much interest to the plant breeder who has produced many stately varieties. The era of immense spikes has passed its zenith and the trend is to develop a range of hybrids not exceeding about 4½ feet in height. These are of much more general use in gardens which are ever becoming smaller, but more numerous. From the glorious shades of blue the colour range has been extended from white and cream through pink, carmine, mauve, lavender, purple and violet. Now, thanks to the work done by Dr Legro, the celebrated Dutch hybridist, the range includes shades of cerise, orange,

1 The flowers of Dimorphotheca ecklonis, a half-hardy South African plant, open only in bright sunlight.
2 Dimorphotheca 'Giant Goliath' produces extra-large blooms.

peach and tomato-red. Our garden hybrids have been mainly derived from *Delphinium elatum*, a natural tetraploid species, but Dr Legro succeeded in overcoming the sterility barrier when he made a number of species crosses at diploid level, tetraploided the resulting plants and then successfully married them to hybrid elatums. The rediscovery of the white African species, *D. leroyi*, which has a freesia-like fragrance, also opens up pleasing possibilities. First crosses at diploid level have shown that this quality is not recessive, so hopes are high, but all this work takes time. In England Dr B. J. Langdon has also been working on these problems and during the next few years we should see a truly remarkable range of hybrid delphiniums.

Dimorphotheca (di-mor-foth-e-ka)
From the Greek *di*, two, *morphe*, shape, *theca*, seed, because the flower produces two different shapes of seed, one from the disk florets and another from the ray florets (*Compositae*). Cape marigold, star of the veldt, Namaqualand daisy. A genus of half-hardy annual, herbaceous perennial and sub-shrubby plants from South Africa, grown for their long-lasting daisy-like flowers in bright colours. Considerable confusion in naming exists in many books and catalogues and according to some authorities those plants known as dimorphothecas should be split up between the genera *Castalis*, *Chrysanthemoides*, *Dimorphotheca* and *Osteospermum*. Here, for the sake of convenience, they are all treated as belonging to the genus *Dimorphotheca*.
Species cultivated *D. aurantiaca* (syn. *Castalis tragus*, *D. flaccida* and apparently the true name for many of the plants grown in gardens under the names of *D. calendulacea* and *D. sinuata*), 1–1½ feet, bright orange flowers with a dark brown disk, edged with metallic blue, June to September, a perennial usually treated as a half-hardy annual. This species has given rise to several garden hybrids (listed in catalogues) such as 'Buff Beauty'; 'Goliath', extra large, mainly orange flowers; 'Lemon Queen'; 'Orange Glory'; 'Glistening White' and 'White Beauty'. *D. barberiae* (syn. *Osteospermum barberiae*), 1½ feet, aromatic foliage, long stemmed rosy-lilac flowers, summer to autumn, with occasional flowers appearing at almost any time, sub-shrubby. This plant is hardier than is generally supposed and will usually survive out of doors in the south of England, making large spreading clumps. There is a dwarf form, *compacta*, which is said to be hardier still. *D. calendulacea* see *D. aurantiaca*. *D. ecklonis*, 2–3 feet, flowers white with reverse of petals purple and a deep purple zone on the petals, perennial treated as annual. *D. pluvialis* (syn. *D. annua*), 1 foot, almost hardy, white above, purple below; var. *ringens*, violet ring round disk, June onwards.

D. sinuata see *D. aurantiaca*.
Cultivation Sun is essential for all species and in a poor cloudy summer, nothing can be done to improve the results since the flowers of most kinds open only in sunny weather, closing or failing to open when the sky is overcast, or in late afternoon. Out of doors they do best in the lighter soils, although *D. barberiae* will thrive on any kind of soil, even heavy clay. In the sunny greenhouse dimorphothecas are grown in pots containing a compost of 3 parts of sandy loam, 1 part of leafmould, plus silver sand. The minimum temperature in winter, when they need moderate watering only, should be 40°F (4°C). Propagation is by seed sown in March in pans or boxes in heat and, after hardening off, the seedlings may be put out in the border in late May or early June. The plants grow quickly and will start flowering in June. Perennial species may be propogated by cuttings taken in late summer and rooted in a greenhouse or frame. *D. pluvialis* is probably the hardiest of those grown as annuals and seed of this species may be sown out of doors in early April in fine soil, the seedlings later thinned, to start flowering at the end of June.

Dorotheanthus (dor-o-the-an-thus)
Named in honour of Frau Dorothea Schwantes, wife of a German botanist (*Aizoaceae*). Greenhouse succulents from South Africa, often found under *Mesembryanthemum*. They may be used for bedding out or as pot plants.
Species cultivated *D. bellidiformis*, dwarf spreading plant, leaves fleshy, flowers open in sunshine, colours, white, pink, red and orange. *D. gramineus*, short-stemmed and spreading, flowers bright carmine. *D. tricolor*, spreading habit, leaves long and curved, flowers white below and purple above. All these are natives of Cape Province.
Cultivation An open compost is needed; out of doors see that the soil is well-drained and plant in sunny positions. These plants are annuals and three plants in a pot make a good display; they do not require high temperatures. Propagation is by seeds sown on seed compost. Do not cover the seed. The temperature should be 70°F (21°C). Keep the seed pans moist and shaded while germination is taking place, prick out the seedlings and grow them on in a frame. The plants should be potted up or planted out in June.

Dorotheanthus (sometimes called Mesembryanthemum) flowers freely at the Karoo Garden, Worcester, South Africa. They need a position in full sun, as they only open in bright sunlight.

1 Eccremocarpus scaber, the Chilean Glory Flower, is a climbing plant that grows well in the protection of a warm wall.
2 Echium vulgare is a biennial that grows to 3 feet in ordinary soil.

Eccremocarpus (ek-re-mo-kar-pus)

From the Greek *ekkremes*, pendant, and *karpos*, fruit, describing the pendulous seed vessels (*Bignoniaceae*). An attractive evergreen half-hardy annual climbing plant. There are very few species and of these one only is in cultivation. This is *E. scaber*, the Chilean glory flower. It grows up to 15–20 feet, clinging to suitable supports by means of tendrils at the ends of the leaves. The flowers, borne in clusters from late spring to autumn, are tubular in shape, scarlet or orange-red and yellow in colour. There is a golden-flowered variety, *aureus*, and an orange-red variety, *ruber*.

Cultivation *E. scaber* is very easily raised from seed sown in pots of sandy soil in March or April and germinated in a temperature of about 60°F (16°C). Seed will even germinate out of doors in milder gardens if sown in April or May. Plant out in June in a light, rich soil against south or southwest facing walls, with trellis, wires, etc., for support. The growths are weak, so that they will do no harm if the plant is allowed to scramble over shrubs. In mild winters the roots are hardy, but in exposed gardens should be covered with old ashes or matting in severe weather. In favoured gardens, the plant appears to be quite hardy except, perhaps, in very severe winters, when it may be cut to the ground only to spring again from the base. Seed is set very freely in long capsules which turn dark brown as they ripen. Self-sown seedlings occasionally appear in the spring, particularly where they have germinated between paving stones and thus the seed has had some protection during the winter.

Echium (ek-e-um)

From the Greek *echis*, a viper, referring either to the supposed resemblance of the seed to a viper's head or the belief that the plant was efficacious against the adder's bite (*Boraginaceae*). Viper's bugloss. Hardy and half-hardy annual, biennial and perennial plants mainly from the Mediterranean region and the Canary Islands.

Species cultivated: Annual and biennial *E. creticum*, 1–1½ feet, violet, July, annual. *E. plantagineum*, 2–3 feet, rich bluish-purple, summer, annual or biennial. *E. vulgare*, 3–4 feet, purple or blue, summer, biennial, native. *E. wildpretii*, 2–3 feet, rose-pink, summer, biennial.

Cultivation Plant out the perennial kinds in ordinary well-drained soil and in a sunny position in May. Seed of the annual kinds is sown in a sunny position in the open in April or August. The perennials are propagated by seed sown out of doors in spring.

Eschscholzia (esh-olt-se-a)

Commemorating Johann Friedrich von Eschsholz, physician and naturalist, member of a Russian expedition to northwest America in the early nineteenth century (*Papaveraceae*). A small genus of hardy annuals from northwest America, bearing saucer-shaped flowers which open to the sun and close up during damp and cloudy weather.

Species cultivated *E. caespitosa*, 6 inches, flowers yellow, 1 inch across, summer; 'Sundew' with lemon-yellow flowers is a cultivar. *E. californica*, the Californian poppy. This grows 1–1½ feet tall and has 2 inch wide bright yellow or orange flowers in summer; var. *alba flore pleno* has double white flowers. There are numerous named varieties and strains to be found seedsmen's lists, in which the flowers vary from the palest lemon and apricot to a clear orange-red. Both single and double varieties are available, in heights from 9 inches–1 foot or so. The foliage is a consistent pale silvery-green, light, feathery and an exquisite foil for the flowers. They will be found under such names as 'Monarch Art Shades'; 'Carmine King'; 'Golden Glory'; 'Mandarin' and 'Toreador'. New strains are constantly being developed.

Cultivation A light, well-drained soil is most suitable, although these annuals will grow in any ordinary garden soil.

Where they flourish they will seed themselves freely. Sow seed out of doors in open, sunny positions in September or March to April where the plants are to flower and thin the seedlings to 6 inches apart, as soon as they are large enough to handle, to prevent them from becoming spindly. Once the flowers begin to fade cut them off to prevent the formation of seed and thus prolong the flowering season unless, of course, self-sown seedlings are required.

Exacum (eks-ak-um)

From the Latin *ex*, out of, *ago*, to drive; the plant was thought to expel poison (*Gentianaceae*). Hot-house annuals, biennials and perennials first grown here in the middle of the nineteenth century for their freely-produced flowers.

Species cultivated *E. affine*, 6 inches, fragrant, bluish-lilac flowers, June to October, Socotra; var. *atrocaeruleum* gentian-blue. *E. macranthum*, 1½ feet, purple, summer, Ceylon. *E. zeylanicum*, 2 feet, violet-purple, summer, Ceylon.

Cultivation Exacums like a compost of equal parts of loam, peat, sand and leafmould and need a minimum winter temperature of 50°F (10°C). Sharp drainage is essential as the plants are particularly liable to damp off. The atmosphere should be moist and shade is needed from hot sun. Propagation is from seed, sown in August and September, the seedlings over-wintered in small pots and potted on into 5-inch pots in March for summer flowering.

Felicia (fel-is-e-a)

From the Latin *felix*, cheerful, a reference to the bright flowers (*Compositae*). Half-hardy annual or greenhouse evergreen plants, some of them sub-shrubs, from South Africa and Abyssinia.

Species cultivated *F. amelloides* (syn. *Agathaea coelestis*), blue daisy, blue marguerite, 1–1½ feet, half-hardy perennial, blue daisies, June to August, an attractive pot plant for the cold greenhouse or conservatory. *F. bergeriana*, kingfisher daisy, 6 inches, half-hardy annual, blue flowers, June onwards. *F. petiolata*, prostrate evergreen sub-shrub, pink to blue flowers, summer. *F. tenella* (syn. *F. fragilis*), 1 foot, half-hardy annual, small violet-blue flowers with yellow centres, July and August.

Cultivation Seeds of the half-hardy annual kinds should be sown in the greenhouse in March in light soil, and the seedlings gradually hardened off and planted out in late May where they are

1 Eschscholzia californica 'Monarch Art Shades', the Californian Poppy, produces semi-double blooms of various shades and flowers over a long period.
2 Exacum affine has fragrant bluish-lilac flowers with prominent golden stamens. It is especially attractive as a pot plant.

to flower. The greenhouse kinds can be raised from seed sown at the same time, pricked off into small pots and then into 5 inch pots in which they will flower. Cuttings of young shoots can be made in spring or August and inserted round the edge of a pot in sandy compost in a propagating case or where a temperature of 55–65°F (13–18°C) can be maintained.

Gilia (gil-e-a)

Commemorating Felipe Luis Gil, eighteenth-century Spanish botanist (*Polemoniaceae*). A genus of annuals, biennials, perennials and a few subshrubs from both North and South America. Although they are attractive plants, few species are in general cultivation.

Annual species cultivated *G. achilleifolia*, 1 foot, purplish-blue flowers; var. *major*, larger flowers, August. *G. androsacea* (syn. *Leptosiphon androsaceus*), 1 foot, white, pink or lilac flowers with yellow throats, August. *G. capitata*, Queen Anne's thimbles, 12–15 inches, lavender-blue flowers, summer; var. *alba*, white. *G. densiflora* (syn. *Leptosiphon densiflorus*), 1–2 feet, lilac or white flowers, June. *G. hybrida* (syn. *Leptosiphon hybridus*), 3–6 inches, various colours, summer. *G. micrantha*, 9 inches, rose-pink flowers, summer, useful for the rock garden and paved paths. *G. tricolor*, 1–2 feet, lavender and white, with dark throats, summer.

Biennial *G. rubra* (syn. *G. coronopifolia*), 3 feet or more, plumed spikes of brilliant red flowers, July to October; colour variations occur in pinks and yellows.

Shrubby *G. californica*, prickly phlox, 3 feet, pink flowers, July. *G. montana* (syn. *Linanthus montanus*), 10 inches, white flowers, summer.

Cultivation Sunny borders out of doors are ideal for the annuals which can be propagated by seed sown shallowly in April. The biennial *G. rubra* can be treated as a half-hardy annual and potted up to flower under glass the same year, but far better flowers result from a sowing the previous autumn under glass.

Godetia (god-ee-she-a)

Commemorating Charles H. Godet, nineteenth-century Swiss botanist (*Oenotheraceae*). A genus of hardy annuals, popular and showy, greatly improved in recent years, related to the evening primrose (*Oenothera*) in which genus they were formerly included.

Species cultivated Few original species are grown, with the possible exception of *G. dasycarpa*, 9 inches, from the Andes, with mauve flowers and steely blue-green foliage, the parent of many lavender-flowered varieties. The original species have been superseded by the garden varieties now available, mainly the results of crosses between *G. grandiflora*, 6–12 inches, a showy plant of compact habit and the tall-growing

G. amoena, 1–2 feet, with loose habit, both variable in colour.

Cultivars include 'Firelight', crimson; 'Kelvedon Glory', salmon; 'Orange Glory', a deeper salmon and 'Sybil Sherwood', salmon pink, orange and white, all 1–1½ feet tall. Double-flowered cultivars include 'Cherry Red'; 'Rich Pink'; 'Rosy Queen'; 'Schaminii', salmon-pink, all 2–2½ feet tall; 'Whitneyi azalaeiflora plena', pink with a crimson blotch, and 'Carmine Glow' about 1 foot tall.

Another kind, tall but with single flowers, is represented by such cultivars as 'Lavender Gem' and 'Lavender', with dark prominent stamens. These probably come from the 2 foot tall species *G. viminea*, from California.

Cultivation Sow in beds and borders in full sun in April; thin according to ultimate height. The tall double-flowered kinds are the hardiest and may be sown in autumn in a well-drained position and will produce spikes of flower up to 3 feet in height the following summer.

Gomphrena (gom-free-na)

Probably from the Greek *gomphos*, a club or wedge, a reference to the shape of the flower-heads (*Amaranthaceae*). A genus of half-hardy annuals of which only one species is cultivated. Its

1 *Gilia rubra is a biennial usually treated as a half-hardy annual.*
2 *Godetia 'Sybil Sherwood' is a summer-flowering cultivar.*
3 *The showy flowers of Godetia bloom in summer.*

Helianthus (hel-ee-an-tuhs)

From the Greek *helios*, the sun, *anthos*, a flower. (*Compositae*). Sunflower. A genus of tall, coarse-growing plants, annuals and perennials, gross feeders, dominating the border in which they are planted. *H. annuus*, the common sunflower, is a plant of some economic importance as the seeds are fed to fowl and produce an edible oil, and the flowers yield a yellow dye.

Annual species cultivated *H. annuus*, 6–10 feet, common or giant sunflower, large yellow flowerheads, late summer, coarse growing; var. *floreplenus*, double flowers. Cultivars and strains include 'Dwarf Chrysanthemum-flowered', 3 feet, golden-yellow, fringed petals; 'Gaillardia flora', 5 feet, brown and yellow gaillardia-like flowers; 'Primrose', 5 feet, sulphur-yellow, darker disk; 'Red', 5 feet, a strain with chestnut-brown flowers; 'Russian Giant', 8 feet, large, yellow; 'Sungold', 6 feet, golden-yellow, double; 'Tall Chrysanthemum-flowered', 5 feet, golden-yellow, fringed petals; 'Yellow Pygmy', 2 feet, double yellow, dwarf. *H. debilis* (syn. *H. cucumerifolius*) 3–4 feet, branched plants with somewhat glossy leaves, yellow flowers, summer. Cultivars include 'Autumn Beauty', 2 feet, yellow, coppery zone; 'Dazzler', 3 feet, chestnut, orange-tipped rays; 'Excelsior', 3 feet, yellow, red zones; 'Starlight', 4 feet, yellow, twisted petals; 'Stella', 3 feet, golden-yellow, starry flowers.

Cultivation The best plants are grown in a stiff loam in full sun. Seeds of annual kinds can be sown *in situ* in April, and to get the largest flowerheads water, and give liquid feeds occasionally up to flowering time. The perennials can be divided in autumn or spring. *H. laetiflorus* needs constant checking to prevent it from dominating the surrounding area, and is best planted in rough corners where it will provide useful flowers for cutting.

Helichrysum (hel-ee-kry-sum)

From the Greek *helios*, the sun, *chrysos*, gold, referring to the yellow flowers of some species. (*Compositae*). Everlasting-flower, immortelle-flower. A large genus of plants ranging from alpines to shrubs, bearing daisy-like flowers. Some are commonly dried as everlasting flowers. Not all are hardy.

Annual species cultivated *H. bractetuam*, 2–4 feet, bracts yellow or pink, summer, Australia; *album*, white, *monstrosum*, flower-heads double. Cultivars and strains of *H. b. monstrosum* include 'Fireball', scarlet, 'Golden', 'Rose,' and 'Salmon Rose'.

Cultivation Treat the annuals as half-hardy, sowing in gentle heat in March, gradually hardening off and planting out in May. Late sowings can be made out of doors in early May. The rock garden kinds all like dry sunny spots with sharp drainage, and make good

---

varieties are usually grown in a cool greenhouse either for pot work or to be cut and dried for winter use. The conspicuous papery bracts of the flowers are their chief attraction.

Species cultivated *G. globosa*, the globe amaranth, from India, a plant 1–1½ feet tall, seed of which is available either in mixed colours or in selected colours including orange-yellow, purple, rose and white. There is also a dwarf form *nana*, 6 inches high, of which 'Buddy' is a purple-flowered cultivar, and seed of a form with variegated leaves is also offered.

Cultivation Sow seed in warmth, either in spring or autumn, and transplant the seedlings to small pots when they are about 1 inch high. Pot on as required in a compost of loam, leafmould and well-decayed manure in equal proportions, with a good sprinkling of sand added. Water regularly and give a liquid feed weekly until the plants flower, always keeping them as near the light as possible. Plants will flower between April and September according to the time of sowing. For winter use in dried arrangements and the like, cut the flowers as soon as they have developed fully and hang them up to dry.

Gypsophila (jip-sof-ill-a)

From the Greek *gypsos*, chalk, *phileo*, to love; the plants prefer chalky soils (*Caryophyllaceae*). Hardy annuals and perennials of great value in both the

---

The purple Gomphrena globosa, the Globe Amaranth, is an everlasting annual from India. Its papery bracts can be cut for drying or used to brighten up a group of pot plants.

border and rock garden; the dwarf kinds also look well in pans in the alpine house. They are mainly natives of the eastern Mediterranean region.

Annual species cultivated *G. elegans*, 1–1½ feet, clusters of small white flowers; vars. *alba grandiflora*, larger flowered, *rosea*, bright rose. 'London Market Strain' and a crimson strain are sometimes offered. *G. muralis*, 6 inches, rose-pink flowers.

Cultivation Plant both rock garden and border kinds in autumn or spring, the rock garden sorts in pockets containing a large amount of mortar rubble or limestone chippings. Although the border kinds like limy soil, they are tolerant of other soils but need a sunny spot with good drainage. They provide useful cut flower material when well grown. Propagation of the annual species and *G. repens* and *G. pacifica* is from seed. *G. paniculata* itself comes true from seed but cuttings of the varieties should be taken in June. These should be of young growth with a heel, 2 inches long, inserted in silver sand with gentle bottom heat. Commercially named forms are propagated by root grafting. Trailing species can be increased by cuttings or by division in spring.

scree plants. The shrubby kinds are rather tender and need wall protection in all except mild localities. Plant in April and fasten the main branches to a trellis or wire support. Prune away unwanted branches early in April. They may be grown as attractive greenhouse shrubs in a gritty compost of sand, peat and loam. Propagation of the perennial species is by division in April or by cuttings in a cold frame in spring, and of the shrubby kinds from cuttings of half-ripened wood in August, inserted round the edges of a pot of sandy soil and put in a cold frame.

Heliophila (he-le-off-ill-a)

From the Greek *helios*, the sun, and *philein*, to love (*Cruciferae*). A genus of attractive plants, from South Africa, mostly annuals, particularly effective when grown in masses.

Species cultivated *H. linearifolia*, 1½ feet, blue flowers, summer, a sub-shrubby plant usually treated as an annual. *H. longifolia*, 1½ feet, blue flowers with a white eye, freely produced on long racemes in summer, annual.

Cultivation A light, well-drained soil in a sunny spot suits the heliophilas and they also make attractive pot plants for the cold greenhouse. The seedlings are raised under glass from a March sowing. Those to be grown on under glass are potted up singly into 5-inch pots in potting compost and those to be

1 The annual Sunflower, Helianthus annuus, is a favourite plant which dominates any border in which it is grown.
2 Helichrysum vestitum, the Felted Everlasting, grows wild in South Africa.
3 Heliophila longifolia is a sun-loving mid-summer annual which produces small blue flowers freely in summer. It is equally effective massed in a sunny border or as a pot plant.

planted out of doors need hardening off and planting out 6 inches apart in May. Alternatively seed can be sown out of doors in May on a well-prepared seed bed.

Heliotropium (he-le-o-tro-pe-um)

From the Greek *helios*, the sun, *trope* to turn; the flowers were thought to turn towards the sun (*Boraginaceae*). Heliotrope, cherry pie. Half-hardy shrubs with fragrant flowers, one of which is treated as a half-hardy annual raised afresh each year for summer bedding.

Species cultivated *H. amplexicaulis* (syn. *H. anchusifolium*) 1 foot, lavender flowers, summer, Peru. *H. peruvianum* (syn. *H. arborescens*) 1–6 feet, heliotrope and white flowers from spring to winter according to cultivation, Peru. Cultivars

include 'Lemoine's Giant', heliotrope; 'Lord Roberts', dark blue, large flowers; 'Marguerite', dark blue; 'President Garfield', mauve-blue; 'Vilmorin's Variety' deep purple; 'White Lady', white.

Cultivation A minimum winter temperature of 45°F (7°C) is required and the compost should consist of 2 parts of loam, 1 part each of leafmould and silver sand. Repot in spring or plant in greenhouse borders where plants may be used to clothe a wall. Prune in February, cutting back the previous year's growth to within 2 or 3 inches of its base. By taking cuttings in autumn or spring a supply of small plants for pot work or for bedding out of doors can be maintained, autumn rooted cuttings usually making the better plants. Pinch out the tops when about 5 inches of growth has been made to produce bush plants. Water frequently and feed before flowering. Standard heliotropes are obtained by stopping at the desired height and side shoots stopped subsequently to form a head.

Helipterum (hel-ip-ter-um)

From the Greek *helios*, the sun, *pteron*, a wing or feather; the seed pappus is plumed (*Compositae*). Australian everlasting, immortelle-flower. A genus of sun-loving annuals and perennials, some of them shrubby, the annuals bearing everlasting flowers excellent for winter decoration.

Species cultivated *H. humboldtianum*, 1 foot, yellow, summer. *H. manglesii* (syn. *Rhodanthe manglesii*), 12–18 inches, pink and white, June to September, out of doors; April to June under glass, Australia. *H. roseum* (syn. *Acroclinium roseum*), 15–18 inches, shades of pink and white with yellow or bronze-copper centres, from July onwards out of doors, earlier under glass; vars. *flore plenum album*, double white, *grandiflorum*, larger flowers, various colours, Australia. 'Red Bonnie' is a bright red cultivar.

Cultivation Seeds are sown under glass in March and the seedlings are pricked out and hardened off, ready for planting out of doors in May. Seed may also be sown under glass in September and the seedlings pricked out, and potted on through the winter to provide spring blooms under glass. Water freely and give a liquid feed weekly after the plants are 6 inches high. Light staking will be required, and a minimum temperature of 45–50°F (7–10°C).

Iberis (eye-ber-is)

From the ancient name for Spain, Iberia (*Cruciferae*). Candytuft. A genus of about 40 species of hardy annual, biennial, evergreen and perennial herbs, from Spain and the Mediterranean region. All the species are easily grown, provided they have plenty of sun in a well-drained ordinary soil. The annuals make a useful addition to the annual border, while the perennials are invaluable as a margin plant, or for rock gardens and pillars where there is no fear of damp conditions.

Species cultivated Annual *I. amara*, 1 foot, white, summer. *I. umbellata*, 1 foot, purple, summer; vars. *albida*, white, 'Dunnett's Crimson,' bright crimson; 'Giant Pink', rose-pink, 15 inches; *purpurea*, dark purple. Shrubby *I. saxatilis*, 4–6 inches, white, tinged purple, May. *I. sempervirens*, 9 inches, white, May; vars. 'Little Gem', 9 inches; 'Snowflake', 1 foot.

Cultivation For summer-flowering species sow the annual and biennials $\frac{1}{8}$ inch deep, in March or April in light workable soil or in August for flowering in spring. Thin seedlings to 2 inches apart. Prevent the ground from drying out or the plants will run to seed. Remove seed pods. Propagate the sub-shrubs by seed sown in boxes in April by cuttings 1–2 inches long in July–October, or by division of roots October–March.

Impatiens (im-pa-she-ens, or im-pat-e-ens)

From the Latin *impatiens* in reference to the way in which the seed pods of some species burst and scatter their seed when touched (*Balsaminaceae*). Balsam, or Busy Lizzie. A genus of about 500 species of annuals, biennials and sub-shrubs mostly from the mountains of Asia and Africa. The succulent hollow stems are brittle and much branched. Few species are now cultivated and those that are may be grown in flower borders or under glass, or in the home as house plants.

Species cultivated *I. balsamina*, $1\frac{1}{2}$ feet, rose, scarlet and white, summer, annual, greenhouse. *I. holstii*, 2–3 feet, scarlet, almost continuous flowering, half-hardy, greenhouse perennial; var. Imp Series F_1, low growing, brilliant mixed colours, in shade and sun. *I. petersiana*, 1 foot, reddish-bronze leaves and stems, red, almost continuous flowering, half-hardy, greenhouse perennial. *I. sultanii*, 1–2 feet, rose and carmine, almost continuous flowering, greenhouse perennial. *I. amphorata*, 5 feet, purple, August, annual. *I. roylei* (syn. *I. glandulifera*), 5 feet, purple or rose-crimson, spotted flowers in profusion, summer, annual.

Cultivation Greenhouse plants are potted in a mixture of equal parts loam, leaf-mould and sharp sand in well-drained pots, during February or March. They do best in well-lit conditions, and require moderate watering March–September, but only occasionally otherwise. They require a temperature of 55–65°F (13–18°C) from October to March, 65–75°F (18–24°C) March to June, and about 65°F (18°C) for the rest of the time. Pinch back

1 Heliotrope, or Cherry Pie, is a summer-flowering plant grown for its perfume.
2 The common Candytuft, Iberis umbellata, is available in various colours.

1

2

1 *Impatiens roylei has attractive red buds and blooms in early summer.*
2 *Ipomoea is a twining climber.*
3 *Ipomoea hederacea is the popular Morning Glory.*

the tips to make them bushy during February. Hardy species do well in ordinary soil in a sunny position, about 6 inches apart. *I. holstii* can be grown as a bedding plant and prefers light shade out of doors; it will tolerate varied temperatures. Propagate by seed in spring, sown in heat for the greenhouse species, and out of doors where the plants are to grow, for the hardy species, or by cuttings taken March to August, and placed in sandy soil in a temperature of 75°F (24°C).

Ipomoea (i-po-mee-ya)

From the Greek *ips*, bindweed, and *homoios*, like, in reference to the twining habit of growth (*Convolvulaceae*). A genus of 300 species of evergreen and deciduous climbing and twining herbs, including the sweet potato, and a few trees and shrubs, mostly from the tropics, Asia, Africa and Australia. First introduced in the late sixteenth century. Some of the greenhouse species, which like plenty of root room, are amongst the prettiest of climbing plants. They do best if planted in borders.

Species cultivated *I. batatas*, sweet potato, 2–4 feet, tubers, edible, greenhouse. *I. tricolor* (syn. *I. rubro-caerulea*), red, summer, greenhouse. *I. hederacea*, Morning Glory, blue, summer, half-hardy. *I. purpurea*, purple, summer, half-hardy. *I. pandurata*, white and purple, perennial, summer.

Cultivation The seeds of annual species, whether greenhouse or half-hardy, should be sown (notch seed slightly with file) 2–3 in a 3-inch pot in a warm house in early spring using a compost of fibrous loam, decayed manure and lumpy leafmould. Otherwise the plants are prone to a chlorotic condition. Transfer the plants to a larger pot as required, without disturbing the roots. Train up a tripod of canes until ready for planting. The half-hardy species may be planted out at the beginning of June in a sheltered border on a south wall. Evergreen ipomoeas may be propagated by cuttings or layers.

Kochia (kok-e-a)

Named after W. D. J. Koch, 1771–1849, a German botanist (*Chenopodiaceae*). A half-hardy annual that is prized as a foliage plant; the small bushes, growing to as much as 3 feet, are green in the early stages, changing to crimson later in the season. They make ideal specimen plants dotted in sunny annual or other border, and they also look well as a low background for smaller plants. Only one species is cultivated, *K. scoparia*, belvedere, seldom grown, and its variety *trichophila*, the summer cypress.

Cultivation Seeds are sown in March in slight heat, and the seedlings pricked out and transplanted into their permanent quarters in June after being hardened off. They also make good plants for the unheated greenhouse.

Lathyrus (lath-eye-rus)

Lathyrus is the ancient Greek name for the pea (*Leguminaceae*). A genus of hardy annual and herbaceous perennial climbers, from temperate zones and tropical mountains. The sweet pea, *L. odoratus*, is dealt with in detail under Sweet peas.

Species cultivated Annual: *L. sativus azureus*, 2 feet, blue, June–July, southern Europe. *L. tingitanus*, 6 feet, purple and red, summer, North Africa.

Cultivation Any good rich soil is suitable. The perennial species are propagated by seeds or by division of the roots in the spring. The annual species are propagated by sowing seeds in spring, either under glass and then planting the seedlings out of doors after they have been hardened off, or out of doors where they are to flower.

Lavatera (la-vat-ear-a)
Commemorating a seventeenth-century Swiss naturalist J. K. Lavater (*Malvaceae*). A genus of some 20 species of annuals, biennials, herbaceous perennials and sub-shrubs, mostly from southern Europe and the Mediterranean region. All bear mallow-like flowers.

Species cultivated *L. trimestris* (syn. *L. rosea*), 3–5 feet, pink, summer, annual; var. *alba splendens*, white. Named cultivars include 'Loveliness', 2 feet, deep rose, and 'Sunset', 2 feet, deeper in colour. *L. arborea*, tree mallow, 6–10 feet, flowers pale purple, summer to autumn, biennial; var. *variegata*, white variegated leaves. *L. cashmiriana*, 5–6 feet, pale rose, summer, perennial, India. *L. assurgentiflora*, 10 feet, purple, July,

1 *Kochia scoparia trichophilia*, the Summer Cypress, is a small annual foliage plant.
2 The Kochias are also called Fire Bushes, because in autumn the foliage turns fiery crimson.
3 *Lathyrus tingitanus* is a climbing annual Pea, closely related to the Sweet Pea.
4 *Lavatera* 'Loveliness' is one of the best of the annual Mallows.
5 *Lavatera olbia rosea*, the Tree Mallow, is not entirely hardy.

shrub, California. *L. olbia*, 6 feet, reddish purple, June–October; var. *rosea*, rose-pink.

Cultivation All these lavateras like hot, dry positions and make good plants for the back of a border. The tree mallow is not entirely hardy and may be cut down by frosts, but it usually shoots up again from the base in the spring. The perennial species are planted out in June from sowings made under glass in February or March in a temperature of 60°F (16°C) or from sowings made out of doors in late spring. The variegated tree mallow is propagated by cuttings taken in mid-summer and kept in a closed propagating case until rooted. The annual species are sown in September or April in the beds or borders where they are to flower.

Leptosyne (lep-to-sy-knee-)
From the Greek *leptos*, slender, describing the growth of these plants (*Compositae*). A small genus of hardy annuals and perennials that deserve to be better known, as they are showy in the garden and good as cut flowers. They are very similar in appearance to *Coreopsis*, to which they are closely related, and are natives of America.
Species cultivated Annual: *L. calliopsidea*, 1½ feet, yellow, late summer. *L.*

There are few low-growing annual plants that can surpass Limnanthes douglasii for summer colour.

douglasii, 1 foot, *L. stillmanii*, 1½ feet, bright yellow, autumn.
Cultivation Any ordinary soil will suit these plants but they like an open, sunny position. Sow seeds of the annual species in the spring in the open ground where the plants are to flower, or sow them under glass and transplant the seedlings to their flowering positions in late May or early June.

Limnanthes (lim-nan-thes)
From the Greek *limne*, a marsh, and *anthos*, a flower, referring to the liking some of these plants have for damp ground (*Limnanthaceae*). A small genus of hardy annuals from California, which deserve to be grown more. They will always have a cloud of bees hovering over them, to which they seem to be very attractive, and a common name for them is the bee-flower. In the right soil they are prolific in their production of flowers and if left to seed, will bloom again in the same year, in September and October. One species only is cultivated, *L. douglasii*, which grows 6 inches tall and has delicate fern-like leaves and shining, lemon-yellow and

white flowers, in May–June. The flower colours have also led to the plant being given the popular name, butter and eggs.
Cultivation Ordinary soil will do, but limnanthes grow best in moist soils. Plants should be given a sunny position and they give good displays if grown in clumps. Propagate by seed sown in autumn and spring where the plants are to flower, thinning the seedlings to 3–4 inches apart.

Limonium (li-mo-nee-um)
From the Greek *leimon*, a meadow, because certain species are found growing in salt marshes (*Plumbaginaceae*). Sea lavender. A genus of annuals, perennial herbaceous plants and subshrubs, hardy, half hardy and tender. Once known as *Statice*, these plants are natives of all parts of the world, particularly coasts and salt marshes. The numerous small flowers, usually borne in branched spikes, are easily dried and are much used for long-lasting flower arrangements. All flower in summer.
Annual species cultivated *L. bonduellii*, 1 foot, yellow, North Africa, strictly a perennial but treated as a half-hardy annual. *L. sinuatum*, 1–2 feet, blue and cream, Mediterranean region; there are several cultivars including 'New Art Shades', a strain containing a mixture of

colours; 'Chamois Rose', shades of apricot-pink; 'Lavender Queen', 'Market Grower's Blue'; 'Pacific Giants Mixed', large-flowered strain in mixed colours; 'Purple Monarch', rich purple. *L. spicatum*, 6 inches, rose and white, Caucasus, Persia. *L. suworowii*, 1½ feet, lilac pink, Turkestan.

Greenhouse: *L. imbricatum*, 1½–2 feet, blue, Canary Isles. *L. macrophyllum*, 1–2 feet, blue, Canary Isles. *L. × profusum*, 2–3 feet, blue, late summer to autumn, hybrid.

Cultivation All the limoniums prefer well-drained, sandy loam and a sunny position. The outdoor species are suitable for borders, the dwarf kinds for rock gardens. Plant the hardy perennials in spring and the annuals in late May. Greenhouse species are potted in the spring and fed occasionally with a weak liquid fertiliser. They require a summer temperature of 55–65°F (13–18°C) and 40–50°F (4–10°C) in the winter. Propagation is by seeds sown in sandy soil in early spring, when the temperature should be 55–60°F (13–16°C). Root cuttings of the perennials can be taken in late winter or early spring and rooted in a cold frame.

Linaria (lin-ar-ee-a)
From the Latin *linum*, flax, referring to the flax-like leaves (*Scrophulariaceae*). Toadflax. Linarias are in the main hardy annual or perennial plants from the Northern Hemisphere; the European plant, once known as *L. cymbalaria*, the Kenilworth ivy or mother of thousands, widely naturalised in Britain, is correctly known as *Cymbalaria muralis*. The yellow flowers of the native species *L. vulgaris*) can be seen on roadside verges, banks and in fields throughout the summer.

Annual species cultivated *L. heterophylla*, 1–3 feet, yellow, July, Morocco. *L. maroccuna*, 9–12 inches, violet-purple, June, Morocco; cultivars include 'Fairy Bouquet', mixed colours; 'Northern Lights', mixed colours, 'White Pearl' and 'Yellow Prince'. *L. reticulata*, 2–4 feet, purple and yellow, summer, Portugal. *L. tristis*, 1 foot, yellow and brown, summer, Portugal and Spain.

Cultivation The soil should be well-drained and rather moist. Sunny borders or rock gardens are suitable positions. Plants can be moved and replanted in autumn or spring. Propagation is by seeds sown where the plants are required to flower, in September for flowering in spring, and in April for summer flowering.

Linum (li-num)
From the old Greek name, *linon*, used by Theophrastus (*Linaceae*). Flax. This important genus contains, besides the economically valuable annual which supplies flax and linseed oil, a number of very decorative garden plants. The

flower colour which seems characteristic of the genus is a fine pale blue but there are a number of shrubs with yellow blossoms, and a lovely scarlet annual. The genus is widely distributed in the temperate regions of the world.

Annual species cultivated *L. grandiflorum*, 6–12 inches, rose, summer, North Africa; vars *coccineum*, rose-crimson; *rubrum* brighter than type; 'Venice Red' is a large-flowered cultivar with carmine-scarlet flowers. *L. usitatissimum*, common flax, 1½ feet, blue, June–July, Europe. Historically this is the world's most famous fibre plant; it was known to the Egyptians. Shrubby: *L. arboreum*, 1 foot, yellow, May–June, Crete.

Cultivation The flaxes are not fussy about soil provided it is well-drained and will do very well on an alkaline medium. The annuals need the standard treatment for this group. Sometimes *L. grandiflorum* is sown in pots in July to decorate the greenhouse in the autumn, but whether grown outside or in, it is one of the best annuals for display.

Lobularia (lob-u-lar-i-a)
From the Greek *lobulus*, a little lobe, a diminutive of *lobos*, the lower part of the ear, possibly referring to the forked hairs on the leaves (*Cruciferae*). A small genus of plants closely related to *Alyssum*. There are four species, natives of the Mediterranean region, but only one of any garden value. This is *L. maritima* (syn. *Alyssum maritimum*), 9–10 inches tall, the well-known sweet alyssum or sweet Alison. Though it is really a

1 The Limonium suworowii from Turkistan has lilac-pink, papery flower spikes which are long-lasting and useful for winter flower arrangements.
2 Linaria reticulata, an annual Toadflax, can grow to 4 feet or more in height.

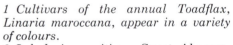

perennial it is treated as a hardy annual
and flowers in early summer. It is a
popular edging plant grown for the sake
of its sweetly-scented white flower.

Some varieties and cultivars are:
minimum, very small-growing, white;
nanum ('Little Dorrit'), compact, short-
growing, white; 'Lilac Queen', pale
lilac; 'Pink Heather', compact; 'Rosie
O'Day', deep rose; 'Violet Queen',
bright violet, very floriferous; *procumbens* 'Snow Cloth', compact mass of pure
white flowers; 'Royal Carpet', very
dwarf, dark purple.

Cultivation There is no difficulty in
growing this fragrant plant, which can
be put in open borders or rock gardens.
Seeds are sown in spring or autumn
where the plants are to grow, and
plants will survive through a mild
winter. Cuttings can be made, but
lobularia will reproduce itself quite
readily from self-sown seeds. It thrives
in any soil, although it does not like a
heavy wet medium one, and prefers a
position in full sun to all others.

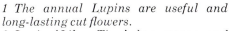

1 The annual Lupins are useful and long-lasting cut flowers.
2 Lupin 'Lilac Time' has mauve and white flower spikes.
3 Lupin 'Tom Reeves' comes into flower in mid-June.
4 Lupin 'Fireglow' is a sturdy cultivar with orange and gold flowers.
5 Lupin 'Whitesheaf' is a cultivar with flat-topped flower spikes which mature from yellow to a deep golden orange.
6 The apricot-pink flower spikes of Lupin 'Harvester' are extra-long.

Lonas (lo-nas)

Derivation uncertain (*Compositae*). There is but one species in the genus, *L. annua*, African daisy, an uncommon and hardy annual, a branching plant, 1 foot tall. The clustered flowers, produced from July to October, resemble those of an ageratum but they are golden-yellow. An added attraction of this Mediterranean plant is that the flowers may be treated as everlasting to combine with other dried material to use as winter decoration.

Cultivation The plant will grow in any kind of soil, but needs a sunny aspect. Propagate by seed sown out of doors in April, where the plants are to flower.

Lupinus (lu-py-nus)

From the Latin *lupus*, a wolf (destroyer), because it was thought that the plants depleted the fertility of the soil by sheer numbers (*Leguminosae*). Lupin. A genus of over 300 species of annuals, perennials and sub-shrubs, mainly from North America, though there are a few Mediterranean species which, since Roman times, have been used for green manuring. This is surprising since the Roman farmers did not know that within the root nodules were colonies of bacteria capable of utilising nitrogen to produce valuable nitrates. The fine Russell hybrid lupins are among the most showy of herbaceous perennials and have a wide colour range embracing the three primary colours: red, yellow and blue. They do not, however, thrive on

1 *Malcolmia maritima, Virginia Stock, is among the simplest of all annuals to grow. It comes in many shades of pink, mauve and white.*
2 *Malope trifida with its shiny purple flowers is sometimes included in the herb garden because of its medicinal properties.*

alkaline (chalky or limy) soils.

Species cultivated Annual: *L. densiflorus*, 1½–2 feet, yellow, fragrant, July–August, California. *L. hartwegii*, 2–3 feet, blue, white and red, July–October, Mexico. *L. hirsutissimus*, 1 foot, with stinging hairs, purple flowers, July, California. *L. hirsutus*, 2–3 feet, blue and white, July–August, Mediterranean region. *L. luteus*, 2 feet, yellow, June–August, south Europe. *L. mutabilis*, 5 feet, white, blue and yellow, summer, Colombia. *L. pubescens*, 3 feet, violet, blue and white, summer, Mexico. *L. subcarnosus*, 1 foot, blue and white, July, Texas.

The annuals are treated as hardy and seeds are sown in drills in April. In May the seedlings must be thinned out to 9 inches apart. It is important with both annual and perennial lupins to remove the forming seed pods before they can grow large enough to retard the flowering capacity of the plants.

The tree lupin, *L. arboreus*, may be raised from seed with extreme ease. These shrubs make rapid growth and will flower in their second season. They are, however, not long-lived, but generally manage to renew themselves by self-sown seedlings. The shrubby lupin, *L. excubicus*, makes a fine large plant,

but needs some frost protection. Like most lupins this has very fragrant flowers.

Malcolmia (often spelt Malcomia) (mal-ko-me-a)

Commemorating William Malcolm, nurseryman, botanist, and associate of the naturalist Ray (*Cruciferae*). Though there are 35 species in this genus of hardy annual and perennial plants, and many quite decorative plants among them, there is one only which is commonly grown, the Virginian stock, *M. maritima*. The vernacular name is a misnomer as this plant is a native of Southern Europe and has been grown in British gardens since its introduction in 1713. *M. maritima*, which is perhaps the simplest of all hardy annuals to grow, is a 1-foot tall plant with a colour range including white, pink, red, yellow and lilac. There is a 6-inch tall variety in various colours, known as *nana compacta*. It is sometimes used to edge beds of annual plants and may be sown quite thickly where it is intended to grow, thinning the seedlings to ½–1 inch apart when they are 1 inch tall. The seeds may be sown in spring for summer blooming, in early summer to flower in late summer and autumn, or in September to bloom in the following spring. Plants may also be grown in 5-inch pots to decorate a sunny windowsill or cold greenhouse.

Malope (mal-o-pe)

The old Greek name for a kind of mallow, meaning soft or soothing, from the leaf texture, or the plant's medicinal properties (*Malvaceae*). This is a small genus of hardy annuals from the Mediterranean

region, with showy rose or purple flowers.

Species cultivated *M. malacoides*, 1 foot, rose-pink and purple, June, Mediterranean region. *M. trifida*, 2–3 feet, purple, summer, Spain; vars. *alba*, white; *grandiflora*, large rosy-purple flowers; *rosea*, rose.

Cultivation Good soil and full sunshine are appreciated and water should be given in dry periods. Soluble stimulants should be given occasionally when the plants are in full growth. Propagation is by seed sown in boxes or pots under glass in March in a temperature of 50°F (10°C), potting the seedlings on as necessary and planting them out 6 inches apart in their flowering positions in May or June. Or seed may be sown ½ inch deep out of doors in April or May where the plants are to flower.

Matthiola (mat-te-o-la)

Commemorating Pierandrea Mattioli 1500–77, Italian physician and botanist (*Cruciferae*). This genus of 50 species is important for the gardener's benefit because it contains those annual and biennial species known as stocks. They are showy plants and most have the additional quality of sweet scent. In the wild state stocks are found in the Mediterranean, Egypt, South Europe and in South Africa, and two species, *M. incana* and *M. sinuata*, are among the rarer British natives. *M. incana* is, in fact, the parent plant from which the annual ten-week stocks have arisen; it is also the parent of the biennials: the East Lothian, Brompton, queen and wallflower-leaved stocks.

The sweetly fragrant night-scented stock, *M. bicornic*, looks a dowdy thing during the daytime but as evening comes the air is filled with its scent. For the sake of its fragrance it may well be grown beneath a window, but not in too prominent a place as it has no beauty of appearance. It is sometimes listed as *Hesperis tristis*.

Species cultivated *M. bicornis*, the night-scented stock, 1 foot, purplish, fragrant, annual, Greece. *M. fenestralis*, 1 foot, scarlet or purple, biennial, Crete. *M. incana*, 1½ feet, purple, summer, biennial. It is from this last species that most of the showy garden stocks have arisen, and any seedsman's catalogue will offer a great choice of colours in various strains. Named cultivars and strains include:

Beauty or Mammoth stocks, all 1½ feet tall 'Abundance', crimson-rose: 'American Beauty', carmine rose; 'Beauty of Naples', old rose; 'Beauty of Nice'; flesh-pink; 'Cote d'Azur', light blue; 'Crimson King', scarlet, double; 'Monte Carlo', yellow; 'Queen Alexandra', rosy-lilac; 'Salmon King'; 'Snowdrift', pure white; 'Summer Night', purple; 'Violette de Parme', violet.

Brompton stocks, mainly 15–18 inches tall 'Crimson King'; 'Giant Empress

Elizabeth', rosy carmine: 'Ipswich Carmine King', 2 feet; 'Ipswich Pink King', 'Lavander Lady', 'White Lady'; *Hybrida* 'Harbinger', early flowering.

East Lothian stocks, 15 inches to 2 feet tall, available in lavender, rose, crimson, scarlet and white and in strains such as 'Giant Imperial', 1½ feet, double flowers in various colours; 'Giant Perfection', 2 feet, mainly double, various colours; 'Improved Mammoth Excelsior', non-branching strain, mainly double flowers, various colours.

Ten-weeks stocks, 15 inches tall, various colours.

Of both Brompton and ten-week stocks, there are available strains known as 'Hanson's Double'. With these it is possible at the seedling stage to select the double varieties as these have light green leaves, whereas those with darker leaves will produce single flowers if grown on. This colour distinction can be emphasised by sowing seeds in a temperature of 54–60°F (12–16°C), lowering it to below 50°F (10°C) when the seedlings have formed their first pair of leaves.

In addition to the above there is a newer strain called 'Trysomic Seven Week Stocks', earlier to flower than all others, which produces plants above 1 foot tall with mainly double flowers in carmine, pink, light blue and white.

Cultivation Ten-week stocks are grown from seed sown under glass in March. Plant out the seedlings in May or June, leaving 9 inches between plants. The soil should be deep and well manured. The night-scented stocks are sown out of doors in April where the plants are intended to remain. The biennials of the Brompton group should be sown in frames in June and July. Transplant when 1 inch high to the places where the plants are to flower in the following year, spacing them 1 foot apart. Or, over-winter them in pots in a frame to plant out in the following March. The intermediate and the East Lothian stocks may be given much the same treatment as the Bromptons but will flower much earlier in the year. Though some seedsmen apply the term 'hardy annual' to many of the stocks, it is in fact not advisable to give hardy annual treatment to any but the night-flowering *M. bicornis*.

Maurandia (maw-ran-de-a)

Commemorating Mme Catharina Maurandy, student of botany, Carthagena, c.1797 (*Scrophulariaceae*). This small genus, mainly of half-hardy climbing

1 Matthiola incana is the parent plant for all the various types of Stocks, which are available in various shades of pink and purple or in white.
2 The Stocks are useful summer-flowering plants. They lend themselves especially well to informal borders and bedding schemes.

Mentzelia (ment-ze-le-a)
Commemorates Chritian Mentzel, 1622–1701, a German botanist (*Loasaceae*). Annual, biennial and perennial plants from North and South America, numbering about 50 species, few of which are in cultivation.

Species cultivated *M. hispida*, 1½–2 feet, yellow flowers in June and July. Perennial which should be over-wintered in a greenhouse or frame with little water at that period, Mexico. *M. lindleyi* (syn. *Bartonia aurea*), blazing star. 1½–2 feet, with golden-yellow flowers and a mass of feathery stamens resembling a St John's wort. The slightly fragrant flowers open only during sunny weather. A delightful hardy annual to be sown in the open in April and May where it is to flower, California. *M. nuda*, 2–3 feet, with creamy-white flowers about 2 inches across borne on slender stems in August and opening in the evening; biennial, for a cool greenhouse, Missouri.

Cultivation The hardy annual *M. lindleyi* does well in ordinary garden soil and a sunny position. The tender species should be grown in pots containing a well-drained potting compost and given little water during the winter. Propogate by seed sown in the spring in a heated greenhouse. Cuttings of *M. nuda* will root if inserted in sand in a propagating frame with bottom heat.

Mesembryanthemum (mes-em-bre-an-the-mum)
From the Greek *mesos*, middle, *embryon*, fruit, and *anthemon*, flower; not from *mesembria*, mid-day and *anthemon*, as is usually suggested. The earliest species known flowered at mid-day, but when night-flowering species were discovered the name was changed to give a change of sense without a change of sound (*Aizoaceae*). These are greenhouse succulent plants, many suitable for bedding out for the summer with a creeping habit of growth, fleshy leaves and brilliant coloured flowers.

Species cultivated *M. albatum*, branching, green and pinkish-red flowers, Cape Province. *M. crystallinum*, ice plant, spreading branches, white flowers, south-west Africa. *M. fulleri*, annual, white flowers, Cape Province. *M. intransparens*, erect stem, white and pink flowers, Cape Province. *M. macrophyllum*, prostrate, violet-pink flowers, Namaqualand. *M. nodiflorum*, cylindrical leaves, white flowers, Africa, the Middle East and California. *M. setosum*, pink and greenish flowers, Cape Province. *M. striatum*, prostrate, white flowers, Cape Province. The plant popularly known as *M. criniflorum* is now called *Dorotheanthus criniflorum*.

Cultivation They should be grown in a very porous compost with ⅕ part added of coarse sand, grit, broken brick and granulated charcoal. The greenhouse kinds require a sunny position with plenty of ventilation in hot weather.

perennials has a few Mexican species worthy of cultivation in the greenhouse. The climbing kinds climb by the aid of their sensitive leaf-stalks, in the manner of a clematis, and are quite suitable for cultivation in a suspended wire basket. The funnel-shaped flowers are large and showy, and their effect is enhanced by the delicate growth.

Species cultivated *M. barcaliana*, to 6 feet, violet-purple, rose or white summer. *M. erubescens*, to 6 feet, rose and white, summer. *M. lophospermum*, to 6 feet, rosy-purple, summer. *M. scandens*, to purple and violet, summer.

Cultivation A mixture of equal parts of loam and leafmould or peat and a little sand suits them. Pots or wire baskets are suitable and these climbers need some sort of support upon which to fix their leaf-stalks, such as trellis work or twiggy sticks. In the growing season

Maurandia scandens is an annual climbing plant which uses its sensitive leaf-stalks to cling to its support.

when plants are flowering, water with a weak liquid fertilizer, but in winter keep the plants nearly dry, with a minimum temperature of 45–55°F (7–13°C). Though perennial, the mauradnias are sometimes treated as hald-hardy annuals. Plants may also be grown out of doors from June onwards in sunny, protected places, such as against south-facing walls. They should be lifted and taken into the protection of the greenhouse in September. Propagation is by seed sown in seed compost in March in a temperature of 60–70°F (16–21°C), potting the seedlings into individual small pots when they are 1 inch high. Cuttings will root in spring or summer in a closed propagating frame with bottom heat.

Give them a minimum winter temperature of 45°F (7°C), and normal greenhouse temperature during summer. Water only when the soil has dried out and keep dry during the winter. Propagate from seed sown in seed compost in March in a temperature of 65–70°F (18–21°C). Do not cover the seeds but keep moist and shaded until the seedlings are pricked out. Also by cuttings taken during the summer and rooted in equal parts of sharp sand and peat. These can then be put out in a sunny position in well-drained soil as bedding plants, or on a rock garden.

Mimulus (mim-u-lus)

From the Greek *mimo*, ape; the flowers were thought to look like a mask on a monkey's face (*Schrophulariaceae*). Monkey flower, monkey musk, musk. A genus of hardy annual, half-hardy perennial and hardy perennial plants grown for their showy flowers. They are found in many temperate parts of the world, particularly in North America.

Species cultivated Annual *M. brevipes* 1½–2 feet, yellow flowers, summer. *M. fremonti*, 6–8 inches, crimson flowers summer.

Cultivation Annual species do best in moist, shady positions, though they will grow in sunny places provided the soil is sufficiently moist. Propagation is by seed sown under glass in a temperature of 55–65°F (13–18°C) in spring. The seedlings are pricked out, and gradually hardened off, finally in a cold frame, before being planted out at the end of May or the beginning of June.

Mirabilis (mir-ab-il-is)

From the Latin *mirabilis*, wonderful, to be admired (*Nyctaginaceae*). A small genus of annuals and perennials, some with tuberous roots, from the warmer regions of America: all those in cultivation are half-hardy plants. *M. jalapa* is unusual in that flowers of different colours often appear on different stems of the same plant.

Species cultivated *M. × hybrida*, 2 feet, flowers white, summer, opening in afternoon. *M. jalapa*, marvel of Peru, four o'clock plant, 2–3 feet, fragrant flowers, various colours, summer, opening in late afternoon, hence one of the common names; 'Pygmee', 1 foot, is a dwarf strain. *M. longiflora*, 3 feet, mixed colours, fragrant, summer, opening in afternoon. *M. multiflora*, 2–3 feet, rosy-purple flowers, summer, remaining open in sun, unlike other species.

Cultivation Sunny positions and quite

1 The Mentzelia lindleyi, Blazing Star, with its glossy yellow flowers, will flourish in any ordinary garden soil and provides bright colour in early summer borders.

2 Mesembryanthemums are multi-coloured creeping plants that are useful in summer bedding schemes.

1 Mirabilis jalapa, the Four O'Clock Plant or the Marvel of Peru, has flowers in shades of deep pink which open in the late afternoon.
2 The wide open blooms of Mirabilis jalapa are especially fragrant in the early evening.
3 The dried calyces of Moluccella laevis are useful for bright floral decoration in the winter.

ordinary garden soil suit these plants, which should be planted out in May or early June, after the danger of frost is over. The tubers may be lifted during October, to be stored, like those of dahlias, in frost-free places in peat, sand, or other material, until they are required for planting again. In the milder localities the black tubers of *M. jalapa* may be left in the ground during the winter and most of them will survive. Quicker results are obtained, however, by growing plants from seed each year. Propagation is by seed sown $\frac{1}{8}$ inch deep during February or March, in seed compost in a temperature of 65–75°F (18–24°C). Young plants should be gradually hardened off, completing this process in a cold frame in late spring to early summer, and finally planted out in June. Overwintered tubers may also be divided at planting time.

Moluccella (mol-u-sel-a)
The name is taken from the Moluccas, islands in the Malay Archipelago, from whence one of the two species is thought to have come (*Labiatae*). Their flowers are curious, the white-veined and enlarged calyces are pale green in colour and look like petals. One of the species, *M. laevis*, is treated as a half-hardy annual and is much sought after by flower arrangers, who grow it specially for this purpose. These flowers are also very useful for winter decoration as they dry well. The 'flowers' have a papery appearance and are green and look like shells, hence the name shell flower or bells of Ireland. The flowers are arranged in whorls along the flowering stem.

Species cultivated *M. laevis*, 1½ feet, white flowers cupped in white-veined pale green calyces, August, Syria, treated as a half-hardy annual. *M. spinosa*, to 8 feet, white flowers, spined calyces, summer, eastern Mediterranean, usually treated as an annual.

Cultivation Moluccellas do best in a sandy loam soil and a sunny position. They should be treated as half-hardy annuals, sowing the seed in heat in February or March. The seedlings are then pricked off and hardened off, ready for planting out in May.

Myosotis (my-o-so-tis)

From the Greek *mus*, a mouse, and *otes*, an ear, in reference to the leaves (*Boraginaceae*). Forget-me-not, scorpion grass. The common forget-me-not is a popular plant for use in spring bedding schemes in combination with other plants such as tulips and wallflowers. There are some 40 species of annuals, biennials or perennials in the genus, natives of temperate regions, particularly Europe and Australia. Those used for bedding purposes are hardy perennials but are usually treated as biennials.

Species cultivated *M. alpestris*, 3–8 inches, azure-blue with yellow eyes, June–July, European mountains; vars. *alba*, white flowers, *aurea*, golden yellow leaves. *M. australis*, 1–1½ feet, yellow,

1 Myosotis, the popular Forget-Me-Not, is a useful plant for spring bedding schemes. Here is it used as a border for a bed of tulips.
2 Myosotis azorica produces mauve-purple flowers in the summer.
3 The dwarfish Myosotis alpestris, with its pale blue flowers with yellow eyes, is a native of the mountains of Europe.

sometimes white, summer, New Zealand. *M. azorica*, 6–10 inches, violet-purple, summer, Azores; var. *alba*, white flowers. *M. caespitosa*, 6 inches, sky-blue, yellow centre, summer, European mountains; var. *rehsteineri*, 2 inches, tufted, April–May. *M. dissitiflora*, 8–10 inches, sky blue, May to July, European Alps; var. *alba*, white. *M. scorpioides* (syn. *M. palustris*), forget-me-not, 6-12 inches, blue flowers with yellow eye, May and June; vars. *alba*, white flowers, *semperflorens*, dwarf. *M. sylvatica*, 1–2 feet, blue with yellow eye, spring, Europe, including Britain, North Asia. Cultivars: 'Anne Marie Fischer', deep blue flowers, compact plant; 'Blue Ball', deep blue; 'Blue Bird', deep blue, winter flowering; 'Carmine King'; 'Compindi', deep indigo-blue, compact; 'Marga Sacher', deep sky blue; 'Royal Blue'; 'Rosea', pale rose; 'Ruth Fisher', very large blue flowers; 'Star of Love', blue, dwarf; 'Victoria', blue.

Cultivation *M. alpestris* requires a lightly shaded place in the rock garden, and should be planted in March or April. Other kinds are best grown as biennials by sowing seed in shallow drills outdoors from April to June. Transplant the seedlings to spring-flowering beds, in October, planting them 4-6 inches apart in ordinary soil. Perennial plants may be increased by division in March or October. *M. azorica* may not prove reliably hardy as a perennial in some years.

Nemesia (nem-e-ze-a)

An ancient Greek name used for a similar plant (*Schrophulariaceae*). Although there are some 50 species in the genus of annuals, perennials and sub-shrubs, mainly natives of South Africa, the majority of plants grown by gardeners are hybrid races and cultivars originating mostly from the South African species *N. strumosa*. These are mainly grown as half-hardy annuals, chiefly to provide bright mixtures of colour in summer-flowering bedding schemes. Cultivars include *N. strumosa*, 'Aurora', 9 inches, carmine and white flowers: 'Blue Gem', 9 inches, pale blue flowers; 'Fire King', 9 inches, flowers crimson scarlet; 'Orange Prince', 9 inches, rich orange flowers, *superbissima grandiflora*, 9 inches, a strain with large flowers in a wide range of

1 Nemesia strumosia suttonii is a selected race with large flowers found in the wide range of colours that characterize this genus. They are effective in a mixed border.
2 Nemesia strumosa with its pale blue flowers is usually grown as a half-hardy annual, producing numerous flowers throughout the summer.

colours. *N. strumosa suttonii* is a selected race with large flowers and a range of all colours found in nemesias. Other hybrid selections include 'Dwarf Compact Hybrids', 9 inches; 'Dwarf Gem Mixture', 9 inches; 'Dwarf Triumph Strain', 9 inches; 'Carnival Mixture', 9-12 inches; 'Red Carnival', 9–12 inches, a tetraploid cultivar.

Cultivation Sow seed in well-drained pans, pots or boxes in the greenhouse in April in a temperature of 55°F (13°C), and transplant the seedlings 1 inch apart in seed boxes until the plants are ready for setting out in the open garden in June, at 4 inches apart. Keep the plants cool at all stages, at a temperature not above 55°F (13°C), and ensure that seedlings are never allowed to dry at the roots nor become overcrowded in their boxes. Seed may also be sown directly into flowering beds, in May and June, thinning the seedlings to 4 inches apart when they are large enough to handle. A sowing under glass in July or August will provide winter-flowering pot plants for the greenhouse. For flowering under glass in early spring sow seed between mid-September and mid-October. Prick off the seedlings first into seed boxes and later pot them on individually into

3-inch pots, finally moving them to 5-inch pots. Forcing in extra heat should not be attempted.

Nemophila (nem-of-il-a)

From the Latin *nemos*, a glade, and the Greek *phileo*, to love, because the plant was found growing in glades or groves (*Hydrophyllaceae*). Baby blue eyes. A genus of nearly 20 species of annual plants from North America of which a few are grown in temperate gardens as hardy annuals.

Species cultivated *N. maculata*. 6–12 inches, flowers white, prominently veined flowers blotched violet, summer. *N. menziesii* (syn. *N. insignis*), 6 inches, spreading in habit, flowers light blue with white centres, summer; var. *alba*, flowers white with black centres.

Cultivation These little annuals are easily grown in any ordinary garden soil. Seeds are sown in March or April, where the plants are to flower in summer, choosing sunny places. Spring-flowering plants are raised from seed sown in August or September, but they may need cloche protection during severe spells. The seedlings should be thinned when young to 3 inches apart. Nemophilas make attractive pot plants for unheated greenhouses or sunny window-sills, if seed is sown in pans or pots and the seedlings into potted-on 3½-inch pots and later into final 5–6-inch pots. Keep them in a cool, shady place until the plants are about to flower.

Nicotania (nik-o-shee-ana)

In honour of Jean Nicot (1530–1600), a French Consul in Portugal, who introduced the tobacco plant into France and Portugal (*Solanaceae*). A genus of some 66 species, mainly annual and perennial herbaceous plants, treated as half-hardy plants, 45 species from the warmer regions of north and south America, 21 from Australia. The most important economic species is *N. tabacum* and its many varieties, grown commercially for the sake of its leaves which when dried provide the tobacco of commerce, although *N. rustica*, still used for this purpose, was the first species used to provide tobacco for smoking in Europe. They all have sticky stems and very hairy leaves, exceptionally large in *N. tabacum*. The long-tubed flowers of the ornamental species are carried in racemes or panicles. The colours vary considerably, due mostly to hybridisation between the white of *N. alata* and carmine of *N. × sanderae*. The flowers

1 The delicate and popular Nemesia is native to South Africa and requires cool, dry conditions before being planted out.
2 The dwarf Nemophila menziesii reaches only 6 inches in height, but because of its spreading growth and profuse flowering habit, it is an ideal summer bedding plant. The light blue flowers have a white centre.

of most of the ornamental species are very fragrant, some of them particularly so at night.

Species cultivated *N. alata*, 2 feet, flowers white with greenish-yellow reverse, very fragrant, summer; var. *grandiflora* (syn. *N. affinis*) has large flowers which are yellowish on the reverse; cultivars include 'Daylight', 2½ feet, flowers pure white, remaining open all day; 'Dwarf White Bedder', 15 inches, flowers remaining open all day; 'Lime Green' 2½ feet, greenish-yellow, popular with flower arrangers; 'Sensation', 2½ feet, a strain with flowers in various colours. *N. glauca*, half-hardy shrubby plant, normally about 8 feet tall, sometimes considerably more, leaves glaucous, flowers yellow, August to October, naturalized in southern Europe. *N. × sanderae*, 2–3 feet, flowers in shades of pinks and carmines, summer hybrid; cultivars are 'Crimson Bedder', 15 inches, deep crimson; 'Crimson King', 2½ feet, crimson-red; 'Knapton Scarlet', 3 feet. Mixed colours are also available. *N. suaveolens*, 1½–2 feet, white flowers, greenish-purple outside, summer. *N. sylvestris*, 5 feet, leaves to 1 foot long, flowers white, long-tubed, fragrant. *N. tabacum*, the common tobacco, to 6 feet, very large hairy leaves, insignificant pink flowers, summer; cultivars include 'Burley', a popular kind for making home-grown tobacco; 'Havana', leaves used for cigar making; 'New Zealand Gay Yellow'; 'Virginica No. 25'. All the above species and hybrids are annuals, except where stated, and all are from north or south America.

Cultivation The ornamental species, grown as half-hardy annuals, will thrive in full sun or partial shade in any good garden soil. The seeds are sown in the greenhouse in a temperature of 55–60°F (13–16°C), in March or April in any good seed compost. The seedlings are hardened off and planted out 1 foot or so apart in June. Seeds may also be sown out of doors in May, where the plants are to flower. In the southern part of the country, at least, self-sown seedlings often appear in late spring. Although *N. alata* is treated as an annual, it is, in fact, a perennial and in sheltered gardens plants may survive through a mild winter, especially if the roots are protected in some way, to flower again the following summer. The roots are thick and tuberous, not unlike those of the dahlia. The common tobacco is also treated as a half-hardy annual, the leaves being gathered in September for curing. For greenhouse decoration *N. suaveolens* is suitable and also the 'Daylight' and 'Sensation' hybrids. The

1 and 2 Cultivars of Nicotiana alata grandiflora have large, fragrant flowers and come in a variety of colours. Because its fragrance is especially strong in the evening, it is very effective when grown under a window.

taller species and varieties need a good deal of space but otherwise make good greenhouse plants. Seeds can be sown in September in a temperature of about 50°F (10°C), the plants being potted on eventually into 6-inch pots. For early summer flowers sow seeds again in February. A fairly rich compost should be used or the plants will be of poor quality. Water plants freely when they are in full growth.

Nigella (ni-jel-la)

From the Latin *nigellus*, a diminutive of *Niger*, black, referring to the black seeds (*Ranunculaceae*). Fennel-flower. A genus of 20 species, natives of the region stretching from Europe to eastern Asia. Those in cultivation are popular, easily-grown hardy annuals with feathery foliage and, in the main, blue flowers though other colours have been introduced in recent years. *N. damascena* has given us the majority of cultivated forms. The dried seed heads may be used for ornamental purposes.

Species cultivated *N. damascena*, love-in-a-mist, devil-in-a-bush, 1–2 feet, flowers blue, summer; vars. *alba*, white flowers; *flore-pleno*, double flowers. Cultivars include 'Miss Jekyll', bright blue flowers; 'Oxford Blue', flowers open light blue and become darker; 'Persian Jewels', mixture including shades of rose, pink, carmine, mauve, lavender, purple and white; 'Persian Rose', flowers open pale pink and become darker seeds of mixed colours are also available. *N. hispanica*, 1–2 feet, deep blue flowers with red stamens, summer.

Cultivation Sow seed in ordinary garden soil, in March or April, where the plants are intended to flower, later thinning the seedlings to 6 inches apart. Seed may also be sown in early September in sheltered borders with a minimum of winter protection, to provide the best plants. If they are raised in a nursery bed, seedlings may be transplanted in spring.

Papaver (pap-a-ver)

An ancient Latin plant-name of doubtful origin, but possibly derived from the sound made in chewing the seed (*Papaveraceae*). Poppy. A widespread genus of 100 species of colourful hardy annual and perennial plants. Poppies like full sun, although some will flower reasonably well in partial shade. The newly unfolded petals have the appearance of crumpled satin and many varieties have a glistening sheen on the blooms. They produce seed freely and many hybrids have been raised which are most

1

2

1 Nigella hispanica has deep blue flowers with purple-red stamens that appear as a dark centre to the flower. They bloom in summer.
2 Nigella damascena, Love-in-a-Mist, gets its name from the way the fern-like leaves surround the flowers.

decorative and easily grown. When used as cut flowers they will last longer if the stems are burned when they are cut and before putting them in water. This seals the milky sap in the stems.

Annual species cultivated *P. commutatum* (syn. *P. umbrosum*), 18 inches, bright crimson flowers with a conspicuous black blotch on each of the four petals, summer, Caucasus, Asia Minor. *P. glaucum*, tulip poppy, 18 inches, deep scarlet, summer, Syria. *P. rhoeas*, corn poppy, 1–2 feet, scarlet flowers with a black basal blotch, summer, Europe, including Britain. *P. somniferum*, opium poppy, 2–3 feet, pale lilac, purple, variegated or white flowers in summer, widely distributed in Europe and Asia.

Cultivation Sow annual varieties in April in patches where they are to flower. They prefer a sunny position and reasonably good soil. Thin the seedlings to 2 or 3 inches apart when quite small. Plant the perennial varieties in October or early spring in deeply dug, loamy soil in full sun, and top-dress with old manure or compost in March or April.

1 Perilla frutescens nankinensis is a half-hardy annual grown for its striking bronze foliage. It is very effective as a summer bedding plant.
2 Papaver rhoeas, the Corn Poppy, is a weed commonly found on arable land. The Shirley Poppies were derived from P. rhoeas.
3 Papaver commutatum is an annual Poppy from the Caucasus and Asia Minor.
4 The summer-flowering Shirley Poppy is an annual with a wide range of colours.
5 A paeony-flowered form of Papaver somniferum, the Opium Poppy, has flowers that are fully double.

Perilla (per-il-la)

Possibly from the native Indian name (*Labiatae*). This is a small genus, containing 4 to 6 species only, of which there is one plant which is of value in the garden. This is *P. frutescens nankinensis*, a half-hardy annual from China, which has been grown by gardeners for the sake of its striking purple-bronze foliage, the margins of which are crisped and fringed. It was much in favour

during the late Victorian vogue for carpet bedding and is still seen today, particularly in public parks. There is a form *laciniata* (syn. *N. frutescens foliis atropurpurea laciniata*), in which the leaves are cut nearly to the middle, and *rosea*, the leaves of which are red, pink, light green and whitish.

Cultivation Seed should be sown under glass in sandy compost during mid-March, in a temperature of 65–70°F (18–21°C). Transplant the seedlings when they are large enough to handle to individual pots and keep the temperature at 55–65°F (13–18°C) until May. Then transfer the pots to a cold frame and gradually harden off the plants until they are planted out 6 inches apart in June, in ordinary good garden soil and sunny positions. The leaf colour of seedlings varies to some extent. To form bushy plants the growing points should be pinched out from time to time. The full effect is gained when plants are massed together.

Petunia (pe-tu-ni-a)

From *petun*, the Brazilian name for tobacco to which petunias are nearly related (*Solanaceae*). A genus of 40 species of annual or perennial herbaceous plants from South America, two of which have been crossed to produce the many named varieties given in catalogues.

Species cultivated The two species concerned are *P. nyctaginiflora* and *P. integrifolia*, from the Argentine, and the resultant plants, though in fact

The brightly-coloured Petunias are among the gayest of summer bedding plants, and although they are really perennials, they are treated as half-hardy annuals in the open garden.
1 The flowers of Petunia 'Moonglow' are yellow, an uncommon colour.
2 Petunia 'Sugar Plum'.
3 A group of mixed Petunias are among the gayest of summer bedding plants.

perennial, are best treated as half-hardy annuals for the open garden. They are handsome plants, very varied in colouring, marking and form, and make extremely effective and colourful displays when used as bedding plants, in sunny situations, during late summer and autumn. Cultivars include 'Bedding Alderman', dark violet; 'Blue Bee', violet-blue; 'Blue Lace', light-blue fringed flowers with violet throat; 'Blue Danube' (F_1), lavender-blue, double; Blue Magic' (F_2), velvety blue; 'Canadian Wonder' (F_1), double flowers, fine colour range' 'Cascade' (F_1), large-flowered, wide range of colours; 'Cheerful', bright rose; 'Cherry Tart' (F_1), rose-pink and white; 'Confetti' (F_2), wide colour range; 'Commanche Improved' (F_1), scarlet-crimson; 'Fire Chief', fiery scarlet; 'Great Victorious' (F_1), double flowers, up to 4 inches across, wide colour range; 'Gypsy Red', brilliant salmon-scarlet; 'Lavender Queen'; 'Moonglow', yellow; 'Mound Mixed', various colours, useful for bedding; 'Pink Beauty'; 'Plum Dandy' (F_1), reddish-purple; 'Red Satin' (F_1), bright red, dwarf; 'Rose Queen'; 'Salmon Supreme'; 'Snowball Improved'; 'Sunburst' (F_1), light yellow, ruffled petals; 'Tivoli', scarlet and white bicolor; 'Valentine' (F_1), red, double, large flowered; 'White Magic' (F_1). There are also strains with fimbriated (fringed) petals in various colours. It is wise to consult current seedsmen's catalogues as very many other kinds are available and new ones appear annually.

Cultivation For growing out of doors, petunias should be treated as half-hardy annuals, sowing the very fine seed carefully in boxes in February or

1 Petunia 'Cherry Tart'.
2 Petunia 'Pink Bountiful' is an F_1 hybrid with rose-pink flowers.
3 This Petunia cultivar has large flowers and fimbriate petals.
4 Petunia 'Cascade' is a popular F_1 hybrid with a wide range of colours.

March in the greenhouse. Use a compost of equal parts of loam, leafmould and sand or seed compost. Make the surface firm, with a layer of finely-sifted compost on top and do not cover the seed with any further compost once it has been sown. Keep the seed boxes in a temperature of 65–75°F (18–24°C) and do not allow the soil to dry out. Transplant the seedlings when they are large enough to handle; begin to harden them off and continue this operation until the plants are set out at the beginning of June. If seed-raised plants are required for increase, overwinter the mature plants in the greenhouse, and take cuttings in the spring, placing them in a sandy compost in a frame in a temperature of 55–65°F (13–18°C). Greenhouse cultivation is similar, but cut the plants back in February or March. Water them freely during the growing season, but moderately at other times. Feed them with a liquid fertiliser twice a week while growing, and keep them in a temperature of 55–65°F (13–18°C) during the summer. In winter do not allow the temperature to fall below 40°F (4°C), and it should preferably be higher. It may be necessary to train the growths, which can be lax and rather sappy, to stakes. For cultivation in hanging baskets or window-boxes or ornamental plant containers it is best to choose such strains as 'Cascade', or 'Pendula Balcony Blended'.

Phacelia (fa-se-lee-a)
From the Greek *phakelos*, a bundle, in reference to the arrangement of the flowers (*Hydrophyllaceae*). A genus of 200 species, natives of North America and the Andes, of hardy annual and perennial plants, of which a number of blue, purple, mauve or white flowering annuals are of great value in the garden. One species in particular, *P. campanularia* has flowers of great depth and intensity of blue colouring, comparable with those of certain gentians.
Species cultivated *P. campanularia*, 9 inches, flowers bell-shaped, intense blue, June to September, southern California. *P. ciliata*, 1 foot, flowers fragrant, lavender, June to September, California. *P. congesta*, 1½ feet, lavender-blue, July to September, Texas, northern Mexico. *P. divaricata* (syn. *Eutoca divaricata*), 1 foot, flowers large, bright blue, July to September, California. *P. grandiflora*, 2 feet, large flowers lavender veined violet, July to September, southern California. *P. minor* (syn. *Whitlavia minor*), Californian blue-bell, 1½ feet, flowers bell-shaped, deep

1 Pharbitis tricolor is a climbing plant with a profusion of funnel-shaped flowers. It is closely related to the genus Ipomoea. 2 Phacelia campanularia, from southern California, bears blooms of deep, intense blue from June to September. It should be sown as a hardy annual in the sunny spot where it is to flower.

violet, July to September, California. *P. parryi*, 1½ feet, flowers cup-shaped, deep violet, July to September, California. *P. tanacetifolia*, to 3 feet, soft lavender heliotrope-like flowers, July to September, California. *P. viscida* (syn. *Eutoca viscida*), 2 feet, flowers deep rich blue with white centre, July to September, California; 'Musgrave Strain' is an improved strain.

Cultivation All the species listed should have hardy annual treatment. Sow seeds thinly in April, where the plants are to flower and thin the seedlings to 6–8 inches apart in June. Any garden soil suits them, and they should be grown in the sunniest position possible. Seedlings transplant badly. As these are hardy annuals, seeds may be sown in September and will generally survive to make excellent plants for early flowering the following summer. Seed is available of most of the species described above.

Pharbitis (far-by-tis)

From the Greek *pharbe*, colour, in reference to the brilliantly coloured flowers (*Convolvulaceae*). This widespread genus of 60 tropical and subtropical, tall, twining, annual and evergreen plants differ only in botanical details from *Ipomoea* and *Convolvulus*, and the species are often placed in the former genus. Those grown are cultivated for the sake of their colourful funnel-shaped or bell-shaped flowers, usually borne in great profusion. It is a remarkable experience to see, in a large greenhouse, the vigorous growths of *P. learii* mounting to the roof and bearing huge clusters of its large, funnel-shaped bright blue flowers, which later turn to pinkish-mauve.

Stovehouse species cultivated *P. cathartica* (E), to 16 feet, purple, August to September, West Indies. *P. hirsutula*, annual, violet to white, Mexico. *P. learii* (E), blue dawn flower, 20 feet, blue to pinkish-mauve, tropical America. *P. mutabilis* (E), blue to purple with a white throat in clusters, South America.

Coolhouse species cultivated *P. lindheimeri*, perennial, light blue, Texas. *P. triloba*, annual, pink or purple, tropical America. *P. tyrianthina* (D), shrubby twiner to 10 feet, dark purple, August to November, Mexico.

Cultivation Stovehouse species grow well in potting compost and should be potted between February and April. A temperature of 65–75°F (18–24°C) is required in summer, and between 55–65°F (13–18°C) in winter. Water generously in the growing season, but moderately at other times and prune into shape if necessary in February.

Phlox (flocks)

From the Greek *phlego*, to burn, or *phlox*, a flame, referring to the bright colours of the flowers (*Polemoniaceae*). A genus of nearly 70 species of hardy,

half-hardy, annual and perennial herbaceous plants all, with one exception, natives of North America and Mexico. Almost all the most important species are from the eastern United States, though the popular annual, *P. drummondii*, is from Texas and New Mexico. The fine herbaceous plants derived originally from *P. paniculata*, the garden forms of which may sometimes be listed as *P.* × *decussata*, have a most important part to play in the garden as they give colour at a time—July and August—

1 The leaves of Portulaca oleracea, Purslane, are sometimes used for flavouring in salads.

2 Mixed cultivars of the annual Portulaca grandiflora, with its spreading habit and bright flowers, are available in a wide range of colours.

3 Primula vulgaris, the Common Primrose, is a native plant that flowers in the spring. Its creamy yellow blooms are found throughout southern and western Europe, and its cultivars appear in a huge range of bright colours.

when it very much needs their bright colours. They are extremely easy to grow and all have fragrant flowers. Our rock gardens would be much poorer if they lacked the various forms of either *P. douglasii* or *P. subulata* or their hybrids.

Annual species cultivated There is one annual. *P. drummondii*, to 1 foot, flowers in a wide colour range, July onwards, from Texas and New Mexico. This is among our most floriferous of annuals.

Annual cultivars *P. drummondii cuspidata* (stellaris), star phlox, 6 inches, flowers starry, mixed colours; 'Brilliant', deep rose with darker eye; 'Isabellina', light yellow; *kermesina splendens*, crimson with white eye; *rosea*, bright rose; *rosea-albo ochlata*, rose with white eye; *nanum compactum*, dwarf strain available in various named colours including blue, pink, red, violet, white. Others are listed by seedsmen.

Cultivation The annual species, *P. drummondii*, needs the standard half-hardy annual treatment. Sow in pans or boxes in March, under glass, and harden off the seedlings and plant them out in June, 6 inches apart. Nip out the points of the shoots to induce bushy growth, and water generously. They make excellent edging plants, and, if allowed to develop naturally, make good plants for tubs, ornamental containers, hanging baskets or window boxes.

Portulaca (por-tu-lak-a)

An old Latin name, possibly from the Latin *porto*, to carry, and *lac*, milk, in allusion to the milky juice (*Portulacaceae*). These are succulent annual and perennial herbaceous plants, with fibrous or thickened roots and small fleshy leaves. Of the 200 or more species in this genus, widespread in tropical and sub-tropical regions, many are considered to be weeds and the group is not very important for garden cultivation. The leaves of *P. oleracea* can be used in salads.

Species cultivated *P. grandiflora*, annual, stems procumbent and spreading, flowers white, yellow, pink, red or orange, June–July, Brazil. *P. lutea*, coarse-stemmed perennial, yellow flowers, summer, Pacific Islands. *P. oleracea*, purslane, annual, a fleshy-leaved plant, flowers yellow, summer, southern Europe.

Cultivation The half-hardy annual species are grown from seeds sown in seed compost at a temperature of 60°F (16°C), and the seedlings pricked off when they are large enough to handle into small pots. Finally they are planted out on rock gardens or in sunny borders in well-drained soil. When grown in the greenhouse in pots, they are placed in very sandy soil and kept in a sunny position, being watered freely in late spring and summer. The temperature in summer should be between 65–70°F (18–21°C), and in winter about 50°F (10°C).

Propagation is by seed, as for most succulents, covered very lightly or not at all, or from cuttings, rooted in sandy soil at any time.

Primula (prim-u-la)

The name is derived from the Latin *primus*, first, referring to the early flowering of some of the species, such as the primrose (*Primulaceae*). A diverse and widely distributed genus of over 500 species including those from the high Alps, moisture-loving perennials and tender greenhouse varieties. All are natives of the northern hemisphere. The one thing most primulas demand is a cool, moist soil containing plenty of peat or leaf soil. Most of the Asiatic primulas —and this is a considerable number of species—are lime haters, but they can be grown in neutral or acid soil, together with the European species. The genus has been divided by botanists into 30 or so different sections, some of which are large and have been further sub-divided, but of these sections, about a dozen or so only are of importance to the gardener. The section to which the species belongs is indicated in brackets after the name of the species.

Hardy species cultivated *P. allionii* (Auricula), 2 inches, grey-green leaves, rose-pink to deep red flowers, March and April, Maritime Alps; var. *alba*, a pure white form; easy plants to grow in pans in an alpine house or cold frame. *P. alpicola* (Sikkimensis), 1–1½ feet, with variable, cowslip-like, fragrant flowers in shades of yellow, violet or white. May and June, Tibet. *P. anisodora* (Candelabra), 2 feet, purple flowers with a green eye in June, Yunnan. The whole plant is aromatic. *P. altaica* (Vernales), of gardens, is now *P. vulgaris rubra*, a pale pink primrose of European origin. *P. aurantiaca* (Candelabra), 1 foot, flowers reddish-orange, bell-shaped, in whorls, July, Yunnan; moist soil. *P. auricula* (Auricula), 3–6 inches, yellow, fragrant flowers in spring and more or less farinose leaves about 3 inches long, European Alps. *P. beesiana* (Candelabra), 1½–2 feet, bright rosy-purple flowers with a yellow eye, borne on erect stems in tiers, June and July, Yunnan. It will soon naturalize itself in moist soil and partial shade. *P. bulleyana* (Candelabra), 1½–2 feet, orange, shaded apricot, June and July, for similar conditions, Yunnan. *P. capitata* (Capitatae), 6–9 inches, with heads of fragrant, violet flowers from June to August, Tibet, Sikkim. Suitable for a moist place on the rock garden. *P. carniolica* (Auricula), 4–6 inches, soft rose-purple, bell-shaped, fragrant flowers

1 *The native* Primula veris, *the Cowslip, is an early-flowering summer plant found in Europe and western Asia.*
2 *Primula vialii bears lavender-pink flowers on long spikes, made more colourful by the red buds at the tips.*

1 The summer-flowering Primula florindae grows best in boggy conditions.
2 The dwarf Primula allionii is only 2 inches high and flowers in spring.
3 The magenta flowers of Primula werringtonensis appear in early summer.
4 The large, pale blue flowers of Primula bhutanica bloom in spring.

in May, Maritime and Julian Alpa. *P. chungensis* (Candelabra), 2 feet, flowers light-orange, bell-shaped, tube red, borne in whorls, June, Burma, China, Assam; moist soil. *P. clarkei* (Farinosae), 2–3 inches, foliage coppery-red, flowers rose-pink, April, Kashmir, rock garden or alpine house. *P. cockburniana* (Candelabra), 1 foot, with dark orange-red, bell-shaped flowers, June, China. Best treated as a biennial in fairly most soil and partial shade. *P. denticulata* (Denticulata), the drum-stick primula, 1 foot, with large, globular heads of lilac flowers from March to May, Himalaya; var. *alba*, is a good white form and 'Prichard's Ruby' is a rich ruby-red; easily grown in moist soil in the border or rock garden in light shade. *P. florindae* (Sikkimensis) 2–4 feet, with large heads of sulphur-yellow, drooping flowers June and July, Tibet. Requires a really moist soil and is admirable beside a pool. *P. frondosa* (Farinosae), 3–6 inches, with rosy-lilac flowers with a yellow eye, April, Balkans. *P. gracilipes* (Petiolares), almost stemless blue or mauve flowers with a yellow eye produced in spring from a rosette of leaves up to 6 inches long, Nepal, Sikkim, Tibet. A charming little plant for the alpine house. *P. helodoxa* (Candelabra), 2–8 feet, with golden-yellow, bell-shaped flowers in June and July, Yunnan. The common name, glory of the marsh, indicates that it likes a boggy place. *P. involucrata* (Farinosae), 6–9 inches, flowers white with a yellow eye in May and June, Himalaya. *P. ioessa* (Sikkimensis), 9 inches, flowers bell-shaped, pinkish mauve to violet, summer, Tibet, moist soil. *P. japonica* (Candelabra), 1½ feet, with purplish-red flowers in whorls in May and June, Japan; var. 'Miller's Crimson' is a striking plant, and 'Postford White' is a clear white with a pink eye. These will seed themselves readily in moist conditions. *P. juliae* (Vernales), 2 inches, forms mats of foliage, flowers, lilac-purple, winter and early spring, Transcaucasia, parent of a number of hybrids, requires moist soil. *P. marginata* (Auricula), 6 inches, with umbels of fragrant, deeply farinose lavender flowers in May, Maritime and Cottian Alps; var. 'Linda Pope', rich lavender-blue with a white eye. *P. minima* (Auricula), almost stemless rose-pink flowers in April, and short, shiny green leaves, southern European Alps. *P. nutans* (Soldanelloideae), 9–12 inches, with compact heads of lavender-blue, fragrant flowers in June, Yunnan. Charming, but short-lived and requires to be kept on the dry side during the winter, so should be grown in an alpine house. *P.×pubescens* (Auricula), 3–6 inches, flowers rosy-purple, April–May, hybrid group; 'Faldonside', 3 inches, flowers rich crimson; 'Mrs J. H. Wilson', 3–4 inches, flowers rich purple with paler centre. *P. polyneura* (Cortusoides), 9–12 inches, pale pink to wine-red flowers in whorls in May and leaves up to 4 inches in length, sometimes hairy, Yunnan, Tibet. *P. pulverulenta* (Candelabra), 2–3 feet, with whorls of claret-red flowers with a darker eye in June and July, China. The 'Bartley Strain' has delightful soft pink flowers. *P. rosea* (Farinosae), 3–6 inches, brilliant carmine flowers in April before the leaves develop, Himalaya; var. 'Delight' is a brilliant carmine-red. For a moist, reasonably sunny place in the rock or bog garden. Once established self-sown seedlings will appear. *P. rubra* (syn. *P. hirsuta*) (Auricula), 3 inches, with rose or lilac trusses of flowers in March and narrow leaves, central European Alps and Pyrenees. *P. rusbyi* (Parryi), 6 inches, red-purple, nodding heads in loose clusters in late summer. The tufts of leathery leaves are lance-shaped and toothed, Rocky Mountains. *P. sieboldii* (Cortusoides), 6 inches, variable rose to purple, with tufts of soft, heart-shaped leaves, Japan, suitable for the alpine

The colour range of Primula vulgaris, the Common Primrose, is quite extensive.

house. *P. sikkimensis* (Sikkimensis), 2 feet, with pendent, funnel-shaped, fragrant flowers in May and June, Sikkim, Tibet, Yunnan. Admirable beside a pool. *P. veris* (Vernales), cowslip, 2–6 inches, deep yellow, fragrant flowers in April and May, Europe, including Britain (rare in parts of Scotland and Ireland), western Asia. *P. vialli* (syn. *P. littoniana*) (Muscarioides), 1½ feet, a slender spike of lavender flowers with bright red buds at the tip in June and July, Yunnan. *P. viscosa* (Auricula) 4, inches, deep violet flowers in one-sided umbels in May, Swiss Alps and Pyrenees. Often confused with *P. rubra*. *P. vulgaris* (syn. *P. acaulis*) (Vernales), primrose, 1–4 inches, creamy-yellow, March and April, western and southern Europe, including Britain. Coloured primroses include: 'Garryarde Guinivere', 6 inches, leaves reddish-bronze, large pink flowers in big heads; 'Garryarde Victory', 4 inches, leaves tinted crimson, flowers wine-red; 'Lingwood Beauty', cherry-red, leaves bright green; 'Wanda', deep

claret-crimson and unnamed blue and pink shades. *P. whitei* (Petiolares), rosettes of ovate leaves, almost stemless pale blue flowers in April covered with farina, Bhutan.

Greenhouse species cultivated *P.×kewensis* (*P. floribunda*×*P. verticillata*) (Floribundae), 9–12 inches, yellow, fragrant flowers in winter and early spring in a cool greenhouse; a hybrid which originated at the Royal Botanic Gardens, Kew. *P. malacoides* (Malacoides), 12–18 inches, whorls of lavender flowers in winter and early spring, China; cars. 'Pink Pride', 8 inches, carmine-pink; 'Rose Bouquet', 15 inches, carmine-rose; 'Snow Queen', 15 inches, white. *P. obconica* (Obconica), 6 inches, pale lilac with a yellow eye in winter, continues to flower for months, China. The hairs on the stems and underside of the leaves are liable to cause a skin rash on some people; var. *alba* is a white form; 'Red Chief', scarlet-crimson; 'Salmon King', salmon-pink. *P. sinensis* (Sinensis), Chinese primrose, 9 inches,

purplish-rose with a yellow eye in spring, China; vars. *alba*, white; 'Dazzler', vivid orange-scarlet; 'Pink Beauty', rose suffused salmon.

Cultivation of hardy species These are best planted in September and October, or March and April, those suitable for the alpine house in pans containing an open, gritty sandy loam with peat or leaf soil in it, are: *P. allionii, P. carniolica, P. frondosa, P. marginata* and *P.nutans*. For waterside planting or in moist soil in partial shade suitable species are: *P. alpicola, P. beesiana, P. bulleyana, P. lentculata, P. florindae, P. japonica, P. pulverulenta, P. rosea* and *P. sikkimensis*. Mulch plants growing in the open with old manure or compost in February. Propagation is by seed sown as soon as it is ripe in a cold frame or by division of the roots soon after they have finished flowering.

Cultivation of greenhouse species Sow seed of *P. malacoides* in June and July on the surface of a compost consisting of leaf soil, loam and sharp sand. Cover the pan with a piece of glass, shade from the sun and germinate in a temperature of 55–60°F (13–16°C). Prick out the seedlings when they are large enough to handle, and when they have grown larger pot them into individual 3-inch pots, harden them off and place the pots in a cold frame. Finally, pot them into 5-inch pots in potting compost and bring them into the greenhouse in September. Keep them in a temperature of about 50–55°F (10–13°C) and feed them with a liquid fertilizer when they are flowering. When potting, allow the base of the leaves just to touch the compost, and pot fairly firmly. *P. ×kewensis, P. obconica* and *P. sinensis*, may be sown from April to August and treated in a similar way.

Quamoclit (qua-mo-klit)

A genus of 12 species of annual and perennial climbers, natives of America (*Convolvulaceae*). They are treated as half-hardy annuals, though *Q. lobata*, at least, is a perennial in its native Mexico. By some botanists they are included in the closely related genus *Ipomoea*. They are grown for the sake of their colourful tubular flowers.

Species cultivated *Q. coccinea*, to 10 feet, flowers scarlet with yellow throat, August to October, tropical America. *Q. lobata*, to 15 feet, flowers crimson quickly fading to white, July to September, tropical America. *Q. pennata*, cypressvine, to 15 feet, flowers scarlet, July to October, tropical America. *Q. ×sloteri*, flowers crimson with white eye, hybrid. **Cultivation** These are tender plants and if they are planted out they must have an exceptionally warm protected spot. They are best grown in the cool greenhouse. Seeds are sown in pots in heat in March or April. Young plants must be potted on and given twiggy sticks as supports. If they are to be planted out of

The unusual flowers of Quamoclit coccinea are scarlet with a yellow throat.

doors, this should be done in June.

Reseda (re-se-da)

Derived from *resedo*, to heal, a name given by Pliny for a species of mignonette which was credited with certain medicinal qualities in healing external bruises (*Resedaceae*). A genus of some 60 species of annual and biennial hardy plants, two of which are decorative in gardens. Sprays of flower cut from the garden in late autumn will keep indoors in a cool room in water throughout the winter and retain their refreshing fragrance. They are natives of southern Europe and North Africa to central Asia.

Species cultivated *R. alba*, 1½–2 feet, a biennial producing spikes of white flowers with brownish anthers from May to September, southern Europe; it is sometimes grown as a decorative pot plant in a cool greenhouse. *R. odorata*, mignonette, hardy annual, 9 inches, with heads of fragrant, yellowish-white flowers from June to October, North Africa, Egypt; vars. 'Goliath', 10 inches, large, very fragrant, reddish spikes; 'Red Monarch', 10 inches, large, deep red heads.

1 *Reseda odorata*, the Mignonette, bears fragrant flower spikes from late spring through early autumn.
2 *Rhodochiton atrosanguineum (syn, R. volubile)* is the Purple Bellerine, a climber with bell-shaped flowers.

Cultivation Seed of mignonette should be sown in April or May where it is to flower, in a sunny position; it is not particular about soil. The seed should be covered with a thin layer of fine soil only and will germinate better when the soil is made firm after sowing. Plants do not transplant readily, but a few seeds sown in a pot will make most attractive cool greenhouse plants.

Rhodochiton (ro-do-ky-ton)
From the Greek *rhodo*, red, and *chiton*, a cloak, with reference to the swollen shape of the calyx (*Scrophulariaceae*). A genus of a single species, a deciduous flowering climber from Mexico, related to *Maurandia*, requiring greenhouse treatment in cooler climates. The species is *R. atrosanguineum* (syn. *R. volubile*), the purple bellerine, which climbs to 10 feet, and has large, showy blood-red, bell-shaped flowers with dark purple calyces, from June onwards, and slender-pointed leaves. The leaf stalks and flower stalks twist round supports, thus enabling the plant to climb.
Cultivation A sandy loam and cool greenhouse conditions are required, or the plant may be grown in the open in warm, sheltered gardens as an annual climber. Wherever it is grown it should be provided with some support such as trellis-work or wire-netting for its twining leaf and flower stalks. Under glass the plant is grown as a perennial, provided a minimum temperature of 45°F (7°C) can be maintained in winter. So treated the plant should be lightly pruned in February, thinning and shortening the shoots and cutting out any dead or dying growth. Propagation is by seed sown in the spring in well-drained soil under glass in gentle heat, or by cuttings taken in August and rooted in a warm propagating frame.

Ricinus (riss-i-nus)
The Latin for a tick, which the seeds are thought to resemble (*Euphorbiaceae*). Castor bean, castor oil plant, Palma Christi. A genus of a single species, which is treated as a half-hardy annual in this country, but is perennial in the tropics. It is much used in tropical bedding, particularly in its coloured leaf forms. Castor oil is extracted from the seeds, which also contain a poisonous alkaloid, ricinin. The species is *R. communis*. The stems rise from 3 to 5 feet high and bear large peltate, palmate leaves which are deeply lobed with 5–12 lobes. The inflorescences are borne at the end of the stems, but the stems branch below the inflorescence, so that the panicles appear to be lateral. The flowers are greenish and unisexual, the males being at the top of the panicle and the females below. The round seed capsules are generally prickly. A number of forms with coloured leaves have been given varietal names, such as *cambodgensis*, with purple leaves and blackish stems; *gibsonii* which is rather compact with dark red stems and leaves; *sanguineus* with reddish leaves, and *zanzibarensis*, with very large green leaves with conspicuous white midribs and which can reach up to 8 feet high. The plant is probably a native of tropical Africa.
Cultivation The seeds, which are large, should be sown separately in 3-inch pots in early March in a temperature of 55–60°F (13–16°C). If higher temperatures can be provided, germination and growth will be more rapid. The plants are kept growing under glass until early June and may require being potted on to 5-inch pots before this. They are then stood out of doors to harden off and are planted out in the open garden about the middle of the month. The plants resent damage to the roots, so if any potting on is necessary, it should be done before the plants

1 *Ricinus communis cambodgensis, the Castor Bean, is grown for its unusual black stems and purplish leaves, and for the seeds, which are the source of castor oil.*
2 *Salpiglossis sinuata, the species from which most cultivars are raised, is noted for the wide range of bright colours of its trumpet-shaped blooms.*

have become at all pot bound. Plants may also be grown in 5-inch or 6-inch pots for decorating the cool greenhouse, conservatory or living room, when they will require moderate watering during the summer.

Salpiglossis (sal-pi-glos-sis)
From the Greek *salpin*, a tube, and *glossa*, a tongue, referring to the tongue-like style in the corolla tube (*Solanceae*). A genus of 18 species of half-hardy annuals, biennials and herbaceous perennials, of which the only species cultivated is *S. sinuata*, sometimes called the scalloped tube tongue or painted tongue, a plant of Chilean origin, which is remarkable for the richness of colour of the large trumpet-shaped flowers and the elegant veining and flushing. It makes an admirable pot plant for a cool greenhouse, and is useful as a cut flower. *S. sinuata* grows 2–3 feet tall and has flowers in shades of rose-pink, crimson, purple, yellow and cream, many of which are beautifully veined. Various improved strains are offered from time to time under such names as *grandiflora*, and 'Splash' is a modern F_1 strain, compact in habit, free-flowering, in a good colour range.

Cultivation Sow the seed in late February or March under glass in a temperature of about 55°F (13°C) in seed compost, and when they are large enough to handle prick out the seedlings singly into small pots of potting compost and grow them on steadily until they are planted out in early June in a sunny border, to flower in late July and August. Seed may also be sown in the open in late April or May where they are to flower. Such plants will come into flower somewhat later than those sown under glass and will thus prolong the display. If they are required to flower in the greenhouse in the spring, sow the seed in July and August and transplant when three leaves have formed, into a 2½-inch pot containing potting compost. Keep them close to the light in a temperature of 55–65°F (13–18°C), and move to 5–6-inch pots when well-rooted. When 6 inches high, take out the tips of the shoots to encourage bushy growth. These fast-growing plants require ample water in dry weather and when grown in a cool greenhouse. An occasional application of liquid fertilizer is also of help.

Salvia (sal-vee-a)

From the Latin *salveo*, meaning save or heal, used by Pliny with reference to the medicinal qualities of some species (*Labiatae*). A large genus of over 700 species of hardy, half-hardy and tender annual, biennial, perennial plants and shrubs, some with aromatic leaves, widely distributed in the temperate and warmer zones. It includes the common sage, *S. officinalis*, a valuable culinary plant, as well as many colourful summer and autumn flowering border plants.

Species cultivated *S. ambigens*, about 5 feet, perennial or sub-shrub, flowers deep sky-blue, September–October, South America, slightly tender, *S. argentea*, 2 feet, most decorative, leaves large, silvery-grey, felted, flowers white, small, in spikes, June and July, Mediterranean region; for a dry soil and a sunny position. *S. aurea*, shrub, leaves rounded, covered with fine hairs, flowers yellowish-brown, South Africa, hardy in mild areas. *S. azurea*, 4 feet, sub-shrub, flowers deep blue, autumn, North America, hardy; var. *grandiflora*, flower spikes denser. *S. fulgens*, Mexican red sage, 2–3 feet, shrub, flowers scarlet, in whorls, July, Mexico, tender. *S. gesneraeflora* 2 feet, sub-shrub, flowers bright scarlet, summer, Colombia, tender. *S. grahamii*, shrub, to 4 feet, flowers deep crimson, July onwards, Mexico, somewhat tender. *S. greggii*, shrub, 3 feet, flowers scarlet, summer, Texas, Mexico, tender. *S. haematodes*, biennial, 3 feet,

The widely-cultivated Salvia has varieties which are used in cooking and medicine, or grown for their beauty alone.
1 Salvia carduacea, the Thistle Salvia, produces unusual bluish-purple flowers.
2 The grey-green leaves of Salvia officinalis tricolor, the common culinary Sage, mature marked with flecks of yellow and red.
3 Salvia farinacea, the Mealycup Salvia, has long-toothed violet-blue flower spikes.

leaves large, wrinkled, heart-shaped, light blue flowers on branching stems from June to August, Greece. *S. interrupta*, 2–3 feet, sub-shrub, leaves 3-lobed, aromatic, flowers violet purple with white throat, May to July, Morocco, nearly·hardy. *S. involucrata*, sub-shrub, 2–4 feet, flowers rose, summer and autumn, Mexico, not quite hardy; var. *bethelii*, flowers rosy crimson in longer spikes. *S. juriscii*, perennial, 1 foot, flowers violet, June, Serbia, hardy. *S. lavandulifolia*, perennial, 9–12 inches, leaves grey, flowers lavender, early summer, hardy. *S. mexicana minor*, sub-shrub, to 12 feet in nature, flowers violet-blue, February, Mexico, tender. *S. neurepia*, sub-shrub, 6–7 feet, flowers scarlet, late summer and autumn, Mexico, hardy in the milder counties. *S. officinalis*, common sage, sub-shrub, 2–3 feet, leaves wrinkled, aromatic, flowers variable purple, blue or white, June and July, southern Europe, hardy; vars. *purpurascens*, reddish-purple stems and leaves, strongly flavoured; *aurea*, leaves golden, flowers rarely produced. *S. pratense*, perennial, 2 feet, flowers bright blue, June to August, Europe, including Britain, hardy; var. *rosea*, flowers rosy-purple. *S. rutilans*, pineapple-scented sage, sub-shrub, 2–3 feet, flowers magenta-crimson, summer, tender. *S. sclarea*, clary, biennial or short-lived perennial, leaves and stems sticky, flowers pale mauve, bracts white and rose, conspicuous, June to September, Europe; various strains are offered; var. *turkestanica*, flowers white, bracts and stems pink. *S. splendens*, scarlet sage, sub-shrub, 3 feet, flowers scarlet, in spikes in summer, Brazil, usually grown as half-hardy annual; vars. for summer bedding: 'Blaze of Fire', 9–12 inches, scarlet; 'Fireball', 15 inches, rich scarlet; 'Harbinger', 15 inches, long scarlet spikes; 'Salmon Pygmy', 6 inches. *S. × superba* (syn. *S. nemorosa*), 3 feet, bracts reddish, persistent, flowers violet-purple in spikes, July to September, hybrid, hardy; var. *lubeca*, identical but 1½ feet tall only. *S. uliginosa*, bog sage, 4–5 feet, leaves shiny green, deeply toothed, flowers azure-blue in spikes, August to October, eastern North America, hardy.

Cultivation Salvias are easily grown in ordinary, well-drained garden soil and in a sunny position. *S. argentea* particularly likes dry soil, as well as sun, and *S. officinalis* should be cut back in spring to encourage new bushy growth. *S. × superba* makes a particularly good border plant when planted in a bold group. *S. uliginosa* prefers moister conditions than the others, and its creeping rootstock should be given a covering of bracken or dry peat in cold districts. Those described as tender will succeed in the milder counties, given the shelter of a warm wall, or they may be grown in the greenhouse in pots in a compost of loam and well-rotted manure or leafmould plus some sand to provide drainage. The pots may be placed out of doors in June and brought in again in September. Water freely from spring to autumn, moderately in winter. Maintain a temperature in winter of 45–55°F (7–10°C). Propagate the shrubs, sub-shrubs and hardy perennial kinds by division in the spring or by soft-wood cuttings, rooted in sandy soil in a propagating case in spring in a temperature of 65°F (18°C). *S. splendens* is increased by seed sown under glass in February or March in a temperature of 60°F (16°C) and planted out in late May or June.

Sanvitalia (san-vit-arr-lee-a)

Named in honour of the Sanvitali, a noble Italian family who lived in Parma (*Compositae*). A genus of seven species, natives of the south-western United States and Mexico, of which one only is in cultivation. This is *S. procumbens*, a native of Mexico, a half-hardy annual, a spreading plant, not more than 6 inches high, with ovate leaves and small daisy-like flowers from July onwards. The ray florets are yellow, while the disk florets are dark brown. A double form, var. *flore pleno* is also known.

Cultivation Seed may either be sown in gentle heat in March and the seedlings planted out after the risk of frost has one, or they can be sown out of doors at the end of May. A sandy loam seems to suit these plants best, but they are not fussy and will grow in most soils, although they will not do so well in very heavy ones. They should be grown in full sun.

Saponaria (sap-on-air-ee-a)

From the Latin *sapo*, soap, the crushed leaves of *S. officinalis* producing a lather when mixed with water, and at one time used as a soap substitute (*Caryophyllaceae*). Soapwort. A genus of some 30 species of hardy perennials and annuals, mainly from the Mediterranean area. They are easily grown, and some of them can become invasive.

Species culvitated *S. caespitosa*, perennial, 3 inches, flowers large, pink on a green turfy cushion of leaves, May and June, Pyrenees. *S. calabrica*, hardy annual, 9 inches, flowers deep rose, freely produced, summer, Italy, Greece. *S. ocymoides*, perennial, 6 inches, a vigorous trailer, flowers rose-pink, on slender, ruddy-brown 2-inch stems, June to August, southern Alps, Sardinia, Caucasus; it may seed itself too freely. *S. officinalis*, bouncing Bet, 1-3 feet, flowers rose-pink, in panicles, August and September, central and southern Europe to Japan, naturalized in Britain. Its spreading roots must be watched; vars. *alba plena*, double white, *rosea plena*,

1 Sanvitalia procumbens is a spreading half-hardy annual.
2 Saponaria calabrica compacta forms small tufts smothered with purple blooms.

semi-double pink, are better garden plants.

Cultivation Plant the perennial kinds from October to April in a sunny position and in deep, good soil. They are propagated by seed sown under glass in early spring, or out of doors in April, by cuttings rooted in a cold frame in autumn, or by divisions of the clumps from October to March. Sow seed of the annual species in a sunny border in ordinary garden soil in April for summer flowering, or sow in the open in September for spring flowering.

Scabiosa (skay-bee-o-sa)

From the Latin *scabies*, itch, for which some of these plants were used as remedies, or from the Latin *scabiosus*, rough or scurfy, referring to the grey felting on the leaves of some species (*Dipsacaceae*). Scabious. This genus of 100 species of hardy biennial and perennial herbaceous plants, mainly from the Mediterranean region, gives a number which are good decorative plants for the garden. The three species which are British native plants, *Scabiesa arvensis*, *S. columbaria* and *S. succisa*, are among our prettiest-flowering wild plants and are quite suited to garden cultivation. *S. succisa*, the devil's bit, is especially good as it has flowers of a bright blue colour. In the plants in the *Dipsacaceae* family the so-called flower is made up of a large number of small florets gathered into a head, or *capitulum*, somewhat as in *Compositae*.

Annual species cultivated *S. atropurpurea*, sweet scabious, mournful widow, pincushion flower, 2–3 feet, flowers deep crimson to purple, July to September, south-western Europe; cultivars include 'Azure Fairy', blue; 'Blue Moon', pale blue; 'Black Prince', very dark purple; 'Cherry Red'; 'Cockade Mixed', large almost conical flowers in various colours; 'Coral Moon', light to dark salmon; 'Fire King', scarlet; 'Loveliness', salmon-rose; 'Parma Violet'; 'Peach Blossom', pale rose; 'Rosette', deep rose and salmon; 'Snowball', white.

Cultivation These plants all do well in chalky or limy soil, which, however, should be enriched. *S. caucasica* is suitable for the herbaceous border, but may also be grown to supply cut flowers, for which purpose its long clean stems make it very suitable. These plants should be lifted and divided every three or four years, moving them in spring as disturbance in autumn can kill them. *S. graminifolia* and *S. ochroleuca webbiana* are suitable for the rock garden. *S. atropurpurea* can be raised from seed sown in February or March in a temperature of 60°F (16°C). Plant out the seedlings in May to flower as annuals, or later disturbance (July) will cause them to behave as biennials. In the latter case, over-winter them in a cold frame and plant out in April. They are good for cutting. Other species may be propagated by division of the clumps in March.

Schizanthus (skiz-an-thus; shy-zan-thus)

From the Greek *schizo*, to cut, and *anthos*, flower, in reference to the deeply cut corolla (*Solanaceae*). A genus of 15 species of showy and attractive annual plants from Chile, sometimes known as the butterfly flowers, or the poor man's orchids. They are suitable for cold greenhouse cultivation or can be sown in heat and bedded out in late spring or early summer.

Species culvitated *S. grahamii*, 2 feet, lilac, rose and yellow, June to October. *S. pinnatus*, 2 feet, violet and yellow, but may be other colours, June to October. *S. retuses*, 2½ feet, rose and orange, July to September. *S. × wisetonensis*, hybrid of first two species, combines their characteristics. Garden strains which have evolved from hybridising include: 'Danbury Park Strain', pansy-flowered, pink crimson, purple and white; 'Dr Badger's Hybrids Improved' large flowers, colours ranging from white and yellow through lilac and rose; 'Dwarf Bouquet', bright rose, crimson, salmon, amber, and pink; Wisetonensis 'Monarch Signal', feathery leaves, cherry red orchid-like flowers.

Culvitation Schizanthus are usually grown as cold greenhouse plants and provide a most attractive display in late winter and early spring. Sow the seeds in August in seed compost in a frame or cool greenhouse, and transplant the seedlings when large enough to handle, to 3-inch pots containing potting compost, giving them as much light as possible, and a temperature of 45–55°F (7–13°C) until January. Then put them in 6-inch pots and grow them in a light position, but do not allow them to become pot-bound. Stop the plants frequently to keep them bushy, and support them by tying them to stakes. In winter they should be moderately watered, but freely at other times, and they benefit from the application of liquid fertilizers occasionally while flowering.

When grown as half-hardy annuals for planting out of doors, seed is sown under glass in February–March in a temperature of 65–75°F (18–24°C). The seedlings are pricked off when they are about 1 inch high, and then planted out in May after being hardened off. They can also be sown where they are required to grow, in May, but require a warm shel-

The unusual blooms of Scabiosa are wild flowers that are easily adaptable to cultivation in the garden, where they frequently behave as biennials.
1 The globular flowerhead of Scabiosa stellata is creamy-white and extremely delicate-looking.
2 The range of colours and cultivars of the annual Scabiosa atropurpurea is quite extensive.

tered site if this is to be done; they will then flower in August.

Senecio (sen-e-see-o)

From the Latin *senex*, an old man, in allusion to the grey and hoary seed pappus (*Compositae*). The largest genus in the plant world; containing between 2,000 and 3,000 species, it covers a wide range of plant types including greenhouse and hardy annuals, evergreen herbaceous plants, climbers, shrubs, an aquatic species and a dozen or more species of tree-like dimensions. The genus is of world-wide distribution. The greenhouse cinerarias are hybrids of one species, *Senecio cruentis* (for their cultivation see Cineraria).

Annual species cultivated *S. arenarius*, 1 foot, flowers lilac, summer, South Africa, *S. elegans*, 1–2 feet, single and double flowers of various colours, summer, South Africa.

Greenhouse species cultivated *S. cineraria* (syn. *Cineraria maritima*), dusty miller, 2 feet, yellow flowers, summer, silver leaves, Mediterranean. *S. cruentus* (syn. *Cineraria cruentus*), parent of the greenhouse cineraria hybrids, 1–2 feet, purple, summer, Canary Isles; many cultivars are available in a wide range of colours from light pink to deep blue. *S. glastifolius*, shrub, 4 feet, flowers purple and yellow, June, South Africa. *S. grandiflorus*, to 5 feet, purple and yellow, August, South Africa. *S. heretieri*, 3–4 feet, white and purple, May to July, Tenerife. *S. leucostachys*, 2–3 feet, yellow, summer, silver foliage, Patagonia. *S. macroglossus*, Cape ivy, climbing, thick, ivy-shaped leaves, flowers yellow, winter, South Africa. *S. mikanioides*, German ivy, climbing, ivy-shaped leaves, flowers fragrant, yellow, winter, South Africa. *S. petasites* (E), velvet groundsol, shrub, 5 feet, yellow, winter, Mexico.

Cultivation of annuals Sow seeds $\frac{1}{8}$ inch deep in patches or drills where they are to grow in ordinary soil which has been previously enriched. A sunny aspect in beds or borders is suitable. Thin the seedlings to 3–6 inches apart.

Cultivation of greenhouse species Use a compost of 2 parts of sandy loam, 2 parts of peat and 1 part of coarse sand and sow the seeds in well-firmed, well-drained compost, in 6-inch pots in April. Use the seed sparingly and cover with sifted compost very thinly. Place the pots in a cool greenhouse, frame or window, and when the seedlings are 1 inch high, thin to 2 inches apart. The climbing species should be given a permanent position where they can be trained up to the greenhouse roof or round a window frame, and the seedlings potted up separately rather than thinned. Water freely during the growing season and feed also, but give little water in winter. The minimum winter temperature should be 40°F (4°C).

Specularia (spek-ul-air-ee-a)

From the Latin *speculum*, a mirror; Venus's looking-glass was the common name of one of the species (*Campanulaceae*). Once known as *Legousia*, under which name they are still known by many botanists, these are hardy annuals from the northern hemisphere. They are much like campanulas. Of the 15 species there is one only commonly grown, *S. speculum* (syn. *Campanula speculum*), a native of Europe. This grows about 1 foot tall and bears purple, somewhat bell-shaped flowers in summer; var. *alba* has white flowers; var. *procumbens* is spreading in habit.

Cultivation Ordinary soil and a sunny position suit these plants. Seeds should be sown in April, thinly, about $\frac{1}{16}$ inch deep. Thin when the seedlings are 1–2

The showy hybrid Schizanthus, known as Butterfly Flower or Poor Man's Orchid, can be grown as a half-hardy annual out doors or makes a colourful display for the cool greenhouse.

1 Senecio elegans, the Purple Senecio or Wild Cineraria, is a native plant of South Africa.
2 The delicate Specularia speculum makes a charming addition to the summer border.

inches high, to 3–6 inches apart. When the plants are over 3 inches tall they should be supported with twigs.

Sweet Pea

The annual sweet pea, *Lathyrus odoratus*, was introduced to England from Sicily in 1699. It was not until 1870, however, that the breeding of sweet peas started to interest Henry Eckford, a Scot, who was a gardener in Gloucestershire at that time. Later he moved to Wem in Shropshire where he made his name for raising sweet peas. The fragrant flowers of the species are in various colours: shades of purple and red, or white and red. In 1901 a new frilled rose-pink variety, 'Countess Spencer' was shown in London and caused a great sensation as it was the first with frilled petals. It was raised by Silas Cole, gardener to Earl Spencer, at Althorp Park, Northamptonshire. Many new varieties were raised and the popularity of the sweet pea became so great that in 1912 a national newspaper offered a prize of £1,000 for the best vase of 12 stems shown at the Crystal Palace. The competition brought in some 35,000 entries.

Of recent years breeding has been continued apace in the British Isles and the United States, and there are now many distinct types in a wide range of colours and heights. The 'Spencer' varieties have the most elegant flowers and are widely grown for exhibition and for decoration. They are available in many beautiful separate colours. The new, early-flowering 'Galaxy Hybrids' produce as many as seven large, fragrant flowers on a stem, many of them opening at the same time. These are also now obtainable in separate colours.

'Knee-Hi' varieties are less tall and grow to about 3 feet in English gardens, although they are reputed to be of shorter growth under Californian conditions where they were first raised. They are free-flowering, with five to seven flowers on quite a long, straight stem which makes them useful for cutting, and they have the advantage of requiring light support only. This is a useful sweet pea for the small, modern garden, or even for growing in a deep container on a reasonably sheltered balcony. The 'Bijou' type do not exceed 1½ feet in height, yet they carry a good crop of flowers and have long-lasting, short-stemmed flowers. With all these types fading flowers should be snipped off, for if they are left to produce seed the flowering season will be much reduced.

Those who grow for exhibition purposes or like to have an early display of sweet peas sow the seed in October, five seeds in a 3-inch pot and over-winter in a cold frame or cold green-house. Once the seed has germinated the seedlings should be ventilated freely except in the coldest weather. Mice can be a menace as they devour the seed and, during the winter, they are liable to eat off the young green shoots, particularly in hard weather when they may be covered in a frame. By making a further sowing in February or March, flowers will then be available over a long period, well into September. Seed may also be sown in the open, where it is to flower, in late March or April, and if the rows are covered with cloches, these will assist germination.

Some varieties have particularly hard-coated seed, and to assist germination such seeds should be chipped. With the aid of a sharp knife a small piece of the outer coat is removed—on the opposite side to the eye—care being taken not to injure the inner white tissue. For a large number of seeds an easier method is to soak them in water for about 24 hours before sowing. This will cause the seeds to swell and any that remain hard can be chipped so that all should germinate about the same time.

Another important point, particularly with spring-sown seedlings is the question of stopping. The growing tip is pinched out immediately when the first or second pair of leaves has opened which will ensure that a strong, bushy plant develops.

Sweet peas are deep-rooting, hungry plants making rapid growth when the days are warm. Therefore they require a deeply dug trench and a rich soil. Those who grow prize-winning stems go to a great deal of trouble in preparing trenches two or three spits deep and work in generous quantities of manure, but perfectly good flowers for cutting purposes can be produced when only the top spit is dug and hop manure, or processed animal manure, obtainable in polythene bags, is worked into the soil. During the growing season oc-casional doses of liquid manure should be given and the plants require ample watering in dry spells.

Plants that have been over-wintered under glass should be planted out in the prepared ground in March or early April, and in some districts it may be necessary to protect the young plants with short pea-sticks or netting against damage by pigeons and other birds. With tall-growing sweet peas the pea-sticks should be placed in the ground

1 Rose-pink Sweet Pea 'Zetra' (left); salmon-pink 'Percy Izzard' (centre) and pale 'Pink Pearl' (right).
2 Unwanted tendrils and side shoots are pinched out of Sweet Pea vines grown by the cordon method.

first and then plant one pea beside each stick, or 8–10 foot cane, if it is intended to grow them on the cordon system for exhibition. However they are grown, the supports should be in a double row 8 inches apart in the row and about 1 foot between the rows. Sweet peas may also be grown on netting, trellis or polythene covered mesh, securely fixed to stout metal or wooden stakes. Where sweet peas are grown in a mixed border the pea-sticks can be in the form of a wigwam with the top tied together so that it will withstand summer winds.

When planting out pot-grown seed-lings, care must be taken not to break the long, slender roots and these should be spread out as much as possible in a deep hole made by a trowel. Or cut the soil with a spade and then firm the soil around the roots leaving the bottom side-shoot joint at soil level.

It may not always be possible to raise one's own seedlings but seedlings may be purchased from reliable sweet pea growers. As stocks of strong seedlings are limited, it is usually necessary to order not later than January for delivery in March. Seedlings may also be purchased at market stalls, but beware of thin, weedy seedlings that may have a yellow, starved appearance through lack of water and poor soil, for it is a waste of time to plant out such miserable specimens.

Sweet pea seedlings are reasonably

The 'Bijou' form of the Sweet Pea is a low-growing type of this eternally popular flower which produces a good crop of blooms on short stems and flowers over quite a long period of time if fading flowers are cut back before they seed.

hardy and will withstand normal spring frosts but perishing east winds can be damaging to newly planted seedlings in exposed gardens and any form of temporary windbreak should be used.

Straw or bracken can be laid along the rows, or hessian or polythene stretched along the canes or pea-sticks. This may appear a little unsightly but it is likely to be required for a short period only, in the early days after planting, and it is one of those little attentions that will make all the difference between success and poor results.

Among the leading prize-winning varieties at National Sweet Pea Society's and other shows, are 'Leamington', deep lilac; 'White Ensign'; 'Royal Flush', salmon-pink on a cream ground;

'Herald', orange-cerise on a white ground; 'Gipsy Queen', crimson; 'Larkspur', pale blue; 'Margot', cream and ivory; 'Noel Sutton', rich blue, and 'Festival', salmon-pink on a cream ground. (See also Lathyrus.)

Tagetes (ta-ge-tez)

From the Latin *Tages*, an Etruscan divine (*Compositae*). A genus of 50 species of half-hardy annuals or herbaceous perennials commonly called marigold, but not to be confused with the English or pot marigold (*Calendula officinalis*). There are now many cultivars with single or double flowers of various forms. They have acquired the names African and French marigold, although the original species from which they have been bred were introduced from Mexico and the southern United States.

Species cultivated *T. erecta*, African marigold, annual, 2 feet, leaves much divided, flowers yellow to orange, 2–4 inches across, July, Mexico. There are numerous cultivars and strains, ranging

in height from 1 to 4 feet, free-flowering, branching plants. A selection includes: 'All Double Orange', 2½ feet; 'All Double Lemon', 2½ feet; 'Carnation-flowered Alaska', 2 feet, flowers pale primrose, to 4 inches across; 'Cracker-jack', 3 feet, golden-yellow to orange; 'First Lady' (F₁), 1 foot, pale yellow, double; 'Golden Age', 2 feet; 'Guinea Gold', 2½ feet; 'Hawaii', 2 feet, bright orange; 'Cream Puff', 1½ feet, creamy-white ageing almost to white, double; 'Chrysanthemum-flowered Super Glitters,' 2½ feet, lemon; 'Golden Fluffy', 'Orange Fluffy', 'Yellow Fluffy', all 2½ feet; 'Collarette Crown of Gold', 2 feet, centre petals incurved, outer petals broad; 'Diamond Jubilee' (F₁), 2 feet, yellow; 'Golden Jubilee' (F₁), 'Orange Jubilee' (F₁), both 2 feet; 'Climax Toreador', 3 feet, flowers mid orange, ruffled; 'Sunset Giants', 4 feet, flowers yellow, broad-petalled. *T. lucida*, sweet-scented 'Mexican Marigold', annual, 1 foot, yellow, August, Mexico, South America. *T. minuta*, annual, 4–6 feet, pale yellow, October, South America, secretions from the roots are said to keep down weeds and research on this is proceeding at present. *T. patula*, French marigold, annual, 1½ feet, leaves much divided, flowers brownish-yellow, July onwards, Mexico. Numerous strains and cultivars are available, in a wide colour range and in heights ranging from 6 inches to 2 feet. These include: 'Sovereign', 2 feet, early-flowering, golden-yellow and brown to brownish-red, double; 'Dainty Marietta', 6 inches, golden-yellow blotched maroon; 'Flame', 9 inches, deep scarlet, double, 'Golden Ball', 1 foot, large flowers, double; 'Gold-laced', 9 inches, dark red, petals edged orange; 'Harmony', 9 inches, centres orange, collar dark red; 'Golden Bedder', 9 inches, double; 'Legion of Honour', 9 inches, yellow, flecked brown at base, single; 'Lilliput Fireglow', 6 inches, dark scarlet, golden centres; 'Miniature Lemon Drop', 9 inches, golden-yellow, blotched maroon; 'Pygmy Mixed', 6 inches, various colours; 'Samba', 1 foot, various colours; 'Spanish Brocade', 9 inches, golden-yellow, tipped dark red. *T. tenuifolia* (syn. *T. signata*), striped Mexican marigold, annual, 1½ feet, yellow, summer, Mexico; var. *pumila*, 6 inches. Cultivars and strains include: 'Gnome', 6 inches, deep orange; 'Golden Gem Selected', 6 inches; 'Lulu', 6 inches, canary-yellow. 'Irish Lace', 9 inches, is a foliage plant, recommended for edging, which makes mounds of slender, lacy-green foliage.

Cultivation Sow seed thinly in boxes of light soil in a heated greenhouse in March or cold greenhouse in April. Prick out seedlings into seed trays when they are large enough to handle and place in a cold frame and after hardening off, plant out, 12–15 inches apart (dwarf kinds, 6 inches apart) in a sunny bed in late May or June. Water freely during dry weather, and give a liquid feed occasionally. Seed of *T. minute* is sown under glass in April and the young plants set out 8–9 inches apart in May, after weeds have been cleared.

Thelesperma (thel-es-per-ma)

From the Greek *thele*, nipple, and *sperma*, seed, referring to the papillose achenes (*Compositae*). A genus of 12 annual or perennial herbaceous plants, very similar in appearance to the genus *Cosmos*, and the generic synonym is in fact *Cosmidium*, but they differ botanically slightly in the inflorescence characters. They are natives of the warmer parts of North and Central America.

Species cultivated *T. burridgeanum*, 1–2 feet, half-hardy annual with a loosely branching habit, flowerheads to 1½ inches across with deep orange ray florets with a reddish-brown basal blotch, June to September, Texas. *T. trifidum*, very similar but the ray florets lack the basal blotch, June to September, south-western United States.

Cultivation Both these species should be treated as half-hardy annuals, sowing the seed in situ out of doors in late May, or earlier, under glass, planting out in June. They grow satisfactorily in ordinary soil, in a sunny position.

Thunbergia (thun-ber-gee-a)

Named after Dr Carl Pehr Thunberg (1743–1822), professor of botany at Uppsala (*Acanthaceae*). A genus of 200 species of twining and dwarf annuals and perennials, mainly from Africa. Most require warm greenhouse conditions.

Species cultivated *T. affinis*, hairy-stemmed shrub, flowers violet, 2 inches across, tube yellow, September. *T. alata*, black-eyed Susan, twining annual, flowers yellow and purple, 1½ inches long but varying greatly in colour, summer; vars. *alba*, white with dark centre; *aurantiaca*, deep yellow, dark centre; *bakeri*, white; *doddsii*, leaves white-bordered, flowers orange with a purple centre; *fryeri*, pale yellow, white centre; *lutea*, yellow; *sulphurea*, sulphur-yellow. *T. grandiflora*, large climber, leaves up to 6 inches long, flowers blue, 3 inches long and across, July to September, India; var. *alba*. white. *T. gregori* (syn. *T. gibsonii*), perennial climber, orange waxy flowers 1½ inches across with lobes half as long as the tube, summer.

Cultivation A well-drained, rich fibrous compost is most suitable. Keep the greenhouse at a minimum winter temperature of 60°F (16°C). Some kinds of *T. alata* will tolerate lower temperatures but it is necessary to maintain the humidity. Propagate from seed, for *T. alata* and *T. gregori* in March–April, or from soft cuttings, using mild bottom heat.

There are many kinds of Tagetes, the French or African Marigold, varying in height and bloom size. All flower over a long period of time.
1 Tagetes 'Cordoba'.
2 Tagetes patula 'Dainty Marietta'.
3 The fully-double Tagetes erecta.

Torenia (tor-e-nee-a)

Named after the Rev Olof Toren (1718–53), chaplain of the Swedish India Company (*Scrophulariaceae*). A genus of 50 species of attractive annual and perennial plants, mainly from tropical Asia, requiring warm greenhouse conditions in this country. The flowers, typified by the well-known *T. fournieri*, are borne in short racemes, with a winged tubular calyx, and corolla with a broad upper lip, the lower three-lobed and spreading.

Species cultivated *T. atropurpurea*, perennial, drooping branches up to 2 feet long, flowers usually single, 1–2 inches long, calyx not winged, corolla tube slender, red-purple, summer, Malaya. *T. baillonii*, low and branched, flowers terminal and axillary, calyx keeled, corolla 1 inch long, upper part red-purple, otherwise bright yellow, Indo-China. *T. fournieri*, erect branching annual, 1 foot, flowers in short terminal racemes, broad wings on calyx, upper part of corolla lilac, lower lip violet, centre lobe yellow-blotched at base, tube to 1 inch long, violet, yellow on back, summer, Indo-China; a number of

1 *Thunbergia mysorensis, a greenhouse climber, produces unusual strands of flowers which hang downward from their support in chains of yellow and orange.*
2 *Thunbergia alata is a popular twining annual with brightly-coloured blooms of yellow and purple. Known as Black-Eyed Susans, presumably because of the large dot or 'eye' in the centre, they flower in summer.*
3 *Torenia fourieri is a summer-flowering greenhouse annual, a native of Indo-China, which produces dainty lilac and violet blooms on upright stems.*

cultivars are available with colour and flower size variations. *T. hirsuta*, annual, spreading, flowers axillary, calyx hairy, not winged, corolla violet-blue with darker tube, India.

Cultivation Species other than *T. fournieri* are suitable for hanging baskets in a stovehouse or warm greenhouse. *T. fournieri* makes an attractive pot plant if supported with slim canes. Sow seed in spring in heat. Potting compost with added organic matter is suitable. Soft cuttings root easily in a propagating frame.

Tropaeolum (trop-e-o-lum)

From the Latin *tropaeum* (or Greek *tropaion*), a trophy, possibly in allusion to the likeness of the flowers and leaves to helmets and shields displayed after Roman victories (*Tropacolaceae*). A diverse genus of 90 species of annuals perennial herbaceous climbers, some tender, others hardy, natives of Mexico and temperate South America.

Species cultivated *T. majus*, nasturtium, hardy or half-hardy annual climber, flowers orange, summer in the wild, Peru; cultivars include 'Golden Gleam', double; 'Indian Chief', flowers scarlet, double, dark leaves; 'Mahogany', mahogany-red, double; 'Orange Gleam', deep orange and mahogany, double; 'Primrose Gleam', double; 'Salmon Gleam', golden salmon, double; 'Scarlet Gleam', orange and scarlet, double; var. *nanum* is a non-climbing form commonly called the Tom Thumb nasturtium. Cultivars of this are: 'Cherry Rose', cerise, rose, double; 'Empress of India', deep crimson, dark leaves; 'Feltham Beauty', bright scarlet, compact; 'Fire Globe', brilliant red, double; 'Golden Globe', compact, double, gold and crimson. 'Jewel Mixed', double, various colours, flowers held well above the leaves; 'King of Tom Thumbs', scarlet, dark leaves; 'Mahogany Gem', deep mahogany-red, double; 'Queen of Tom Thumbs', various, silver-variegated leaves; 'Rosy Morn', rose-scarlet; 'Vesuvius', salmon-rose, dark leaves. *T. peltophorum* (syn. *T. lobbianum*), hardy or half-hardy annual or perennial climber, flowers yellow or orange, summer, Chile, Argentine. *T. peregrinum*, Canary creeper, 3–10 feet, half-hardy annual or

1 Mixed Nasturtiums, Tropaeolum majus, are half-hardy annuals which include both climbing and dwarf varieties and cultivars. They flourish in a poor soil, provided the position is well-drained and sunny.

2 Tropaeolum peregrinum, the Canary Creeper, is grown as a half-hardy annual climber in cooler climates. It is a perennial in mild areas.

3 Ursinia speciosa is an annual with yellow daisy-like flowers.

4 Ursinia anethoides is a native of South Africa.

perennial climber in mild districts, flowers golden-yellow fringed, July onwards, entirely different from the common nasturtium, and requiring a richer soil, Peru. *T. speciosum*, flame nasturtium, hardy perennial, 6–9 feet when established and climbing through a shrub or hedge, flowers brilliant scarlet, June to September, Chile. *T. tuberosum*, tuberous-rooted perennial, 4–5 feet, flowers orange-scarlet, September, Peru.

Cultivation The annual nasturtiums should be sown in spring where they are to flower, in well drained soil and a sunny position. The young seedlings are tender and are liable to frost damage, therefore nothing is gained by sowing before the end of April or later in cold districts, although following mild winters self-sown seedlings often appear. Sow *T. peregrinum* in light soil under glass in March with a temperature of 50°F (10°C), and harden off the seedlings before planting out against a fence or wall in mid-May. It does well on a north-facing wall. The perennial species like a well-drained loamy soil, *T. speciosum* thriving in a cool, north-facing aspect beside a wall on which there are plants up which it can clamber. It does best in the north, where it is often seen scrambling into yew hedges. *T. tuberosum* does best in poorish, lime-free soil and a sunny position; the tubers should be planted in March or April and in colder districts lifted in autumn and stored in the same way as dahlia tubers. *T. speciosum* is raised from seed, although seed is difficult to germinate. The seedlings are best grown on in separate pots as they can prove tricky to transplant.

Ursinia (ur-sin-ee-a)

Commemorating Johann Ursinus of Regensburg (1608–66), author of *Arboretum Biblicum* (Compositae). A genus of 80 species of annuals, herbaceous perennials or sub-shrubs, natives of South Africa, with one species found in Abyssinia. Those grown in Britain are treated as half-hardy annuals. The daisy-like flowers, in shades of orange and yellow, remain open through the day which is not true of all South African annuals.

Species cultivated *U. anethoides* (syn. *Sphenogyne anethoides*), 1–2 feet, flowers bright orange-yellow with a central zone of deep purple, July to September; the cultivar 'Aurora' is bright orange with conspicuous crimson-red base. *U. versicolor* (syn. *U. pulchra*), 9 inches, flowers orange with dark centre, summer; the cultivar 'Golden Bedder' is light orange with deeper orange centre.

Cultivation These brightly coloured daisy-like plants require a light well-drained soil and full sun. They associate well with arctotis, as in the wild in Cape Province. Sow the seed under glass in late March and plant out in mid-May, or when the danger of frost is past.

Venidio-arctotis
(ven-id-ee-o-ark-to-tis)

A bigeneric hybrid (between the genera *Venidium* and *Arctotis*) which originated in England; slightly tender, with daisy-like flowers like *Arctotis*, in shades of orange, yellow, bronze, rose-pink, mahogany-crimson and ivory white. The flowers are borne erect on stems 1½–2 feet high and open during sunny periods only. The individual flowers are short lived but are produced in succession from June to October.

Cultivation The hybrid is sterile and has no seed, and must be propagated by cuttings, the stock plants being lifted and over-wintered in a frost-free greenhouse or frame. Cuttings taken in the autumn or spring may be rooted in sandy soil in a propagating frame and planted out in a sunny bed in well-drained soil in late May or early June or used as pot plants for a cool greenhouse.

Venidium (ven-id-e-um)

Possibly from the Latin *vena*, a vein, referring to the ribbed fruits (*Compositae*). A genus of up to 30 species of South African half-hardy annuals and perennials.

Species cultivated *V. decurrens*, 1½ feet, flowers orange-yellow with a paler zone around a dark disc, July to October, perennial, best treated as a half-hardy annual. *V. fastuosum*, Namaqualand daisy, 2–3 feet, flowers orange, to 5 inches across, with a dark purple zone around a shining black central disc, June to September, annual; the strain 'Dwarf Hybrids', 15 inches, is available in shades of cream, ivory, yellow and orange with black centres and maroon markings at the base of the petals.

Cultivation Sow seed in a cool greenhouse in April, and prick off into small pots and plant out in late May or early June, in a sunny position in a soil that is not too rich. Seed may also be sown in the open in late April where plants are to flower. Germination is often erratic.

Verbena (ver-be-na)

Possibly from the Latin *verbenae*, the sacred branches of laurel, myrtle or olive, or a corruption of the Celtic name *fervain* for *V. officinalis* (*Verbenaceae*). A genus of 250 species of half-hardy perennials and annuals, widely distributed, notable for the bright colouring of the flowers. Those described are from South America.

Species cultivated *V. bonariensis*, perennial, 3–6 feet, flowers purple-lilac, July to October. *V. corymbosa*, perennial, 3 feet, flowers heliotrope-blue in dense, terminal heads, late summer. *V. × hybrida*, florist's verbena, to 1 foot, hybrid, summer bedding plant, many cultivars with flowers in shades of blue, red, pink, many with white eyes, also pure white. *V. peruviana* (syn. *V. chamaedrifolia*), half-hardy perennial, semi-prostrate, flowers brilliant scarlet,

1 Venidio-arctotis is a slightly tender bigeneric hybrid.
2 Venidium fastuosum, the Namaqualand Daisy, has large orange daisy-like blooms with a dark zone around their central discs.
3 Venidium decurrens is a South African perennial best treated as a half-hardy annual.

July to October, bedding plant. *V. rigida* (syn. *V. venosa*), perennial, 1½–2 feet, flowers claret-purple to violet, July to October; cultivars include: 'Amethyst', 1 foot, blue; 'Blaze', 9 inches, scarlet; 'Compliment' 1 foot, pink with yellow eye; 'Miss Susie Double', 9 inches, salmon pink, double; 'Olympia Strain', 9 inches, various colours; 'Ellen Wilmott', 1 foot, salmon-pink with white eye; 'Rose Queen', 1 foot; 'Royal Blue', 1 foot, blue with white eye; 'Scarlet Queen', 1 foot, scarlet with white eye; 'Snow Queen', 1 foot, white eye. *V. tenera*, trailing, South America; var.

maonettii, reddish-violet and white, summer. *V. tenuisecta*, moss verbena, trailing, flowers in shades of blue, summer.

Cultivation Plant in spring in ordinary well-drained soil in a sunny position. In cold districts *V. bonariensis*, *V. corymbosa* and *V. rigida*, should be lifted and over-wintered in boxes of ordinary soil in a frost-free place. In March they should be started into growth in a temperature of 55°F (13°C) and the roots divided when new growth begins. Pot these and plant out in late May. Cuttings of *V. peruviana* should be rooted in late summer in boxes of sandy soil and over-wintered in a frost-free place. *V. bonariensis* is raised from seed sown outdoors in spring. Seed of half-hardy annual hybrids should be sown under glass in February; after the seedlings have been hardened off, plant them out in mid-May.

Verbesina (ver-be-see-na)

Possibly referring to the verbena-like foliage of some species (*Compositae*). A genus of 150 species of hardy and half-hardy annuals and perennials, from the warmer parts of the Americas.

Species cultivated *V. encelioides* (syn. *Ximenesia encelioides*), tender annual, 2–3 feet, greyish, hairy foliage, flowers yellow, August. *V. virginica*, hardy perennial, 2 feet, leaves downy, flowers white, August.

Cultivation These plants do well in a rich loamy soil. Propagation is by seed, or by division of the perennials.

Xeranthemum (zer-an-them-um)

From the Greek, *xeros*, dry, and *anthos*, a flower (*Compositae*). A genus of six species of hardy annuals with dry, daisy-like 'everlasting' flowers, found from the Mediterranean area to south-western Asia. The only species to be cultivated is *X. annuum*, 2 feet tall, flowers purple, summer; vars. *ligulosum*, flowers semi-double; *perligulosum* (syn. *X. superbissimum*), flowers very double. Seed is usually obtainable of single and double flowering kinds in various colours. They are very suitable for winter decoration.

Cultivation These annuals will grow in ordinary soil in a sunny position. Seeds should be sown in light soil in the greenhouse in a temperature of 50–55°F (10–13°C) and the seedlings planted out in June; or seed may be sown in the open ground at the end of April. It is best to thin to about 6–8 inches apart and some support with short hazel twigs is an advantage. As soon as the flowers are fully expanded they may be gathered for winter decoration.

Zea (zee-a)

An old Greek name, possibly from *Zea*, a kind of corn (*Gramineae*). A genus of a single species, *Z. mays*, maize, Indian corn, mealies, etc., a grass of great economic importance in many parts of the world. It is treated as a half-hardy annual and certain varieties are grown for ornamental purposes. These include vars. *gracillima*, 3 feet, leaves narrow; *gracillima variegata*, leaves striped white; *japonica*, 4 feet, leaves striped white; *japonica tricolor*, 5 feet, leaves striped white, yellow and rose.

Zinnia (zi-nee-a)

Commemorating Johann Gottfried Zinn (1727–59), a German professor of botany (*Compositae*). A genus of 20 species of half-hardy annuals and perennials with beautiful flowers of various colours, natives of the southern United States to Brazil and Chile.

Species cultivated *Z. elegans*, 2–3 feet, flowers of various colours, summer; cultivars and strains are numerous; they include 'Aztec', bright orange; 'Big Snowman', white; 'Envy', green; 'Ice Cream', pure white; 'Chrysanthemum-flowered Hybrids', various colours; 'Giant Dahlia-flowered Strain', various colours; 'Mammoth', various colours;

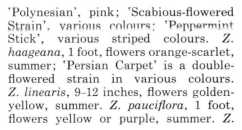

1 Verbena rigida has claret-purple blooms in summer and autumn and is a good plant for mild climates.
2 Verbena peruviana is a half-hardy bedding plant with brilliant red flowers.
3 Verbesina encelioides is a tender greenhouse annual with daisy-like blooms and leaves similar to those of verbena.
4 Xeranthemum annuum produces everlasting purple flowers in summer.

'Polynesian', pink; 'Scabious-flowered Strain', various colours; 'Peppermint Stick', various striped colours. *Z. haageana*, 1 foot, flowers orange-scarlet, summer; 'Persian Carpet' is a double-flowered strain in various colours. *Z. linearis*, 9–12 inches, flowers golden-yellow, summer. *Z. pauciflora*, 1 foot, flowers yellow or purple, summer. *Z.*

tenuiflora (syn. *Z. multiflora*), 2 feet, flowers scarlet, summer. Other strains and cultivars include 'Button-flowered Mixed', 1½ feet; 'Pink Buttons', 1 foot, salmon-pink; 'Red Buttons', 1 foot, bright scarlet; 'Thumbelina', 6 inches, flowers semi-double or double in various colours.

Cultivation Zinnias do best in deep, loamy soil with decayed manure added, in sunny beds and borders. Sow seed in early April $\frac{1}{16}$ inch deep in light soil in a greenhouse, in a temperature of 55°F (13°C) and transplant the seedlings when the third leaf forms, 2 inches

1

2

3

4

apart in shallow boxes. When established they should be removed to a cooler house and then planted out in early May, 4 inches apart in a cold frame, gradually hardened off and finally planted out in early June, 8–12 inches apart. Seed may be sown directly out of doors in May and this has the advantage that the seedlings can grow undisturbed. Rapid changes of temperature should be avoided and the plants should be freely watered in dry weather. The taller species may be staked in windy conditions, as the blooms produced are often double and very big. When flowering starts the application of stimulants is helpful to the blooms.

Zinnias, bright-coloured flowers of summer named to commemorate a German professor of botany, are available in a wide variety of colours.
1 Zinnia 'Old Mexico' is a small, two-coloured double form.
2 Zinnia 'Early Wonder Serenata' has small blooms.
3 Zinnia haageana 'Persian Carpet' produces double flowers in various colours.
4 Zea gracillima, variegated Maize, grown chiefly for its foliage, is grouped with Tagetes, the African Marigold, and mixed antirrhinum tetra to make an excellent summer bedding collection. The Maize grows to about 3 feet in height and makes a pleasing foil for the flower colours.

A Selection of Hardy Annuals

Botanical Name	Common Name	Height inches	Colour
Althaea	Annual Hollyhock	48–60	various
Anagallis linifolia	Pimpernel	6	blue, red
Argemone	Prickly Poppy	24	yellow, orange, white
Calendula officinalis	Pot Marigold	24	orange, yellow
Centaurea cyanus	Cornflower	12–30	various
Centaurea moschata	Sweet Sultan	18–24	various
Chrysanthemum carinatum	Tricoloured Chrysanthemum	24	various
Chrysanthemum coronarium	Crown Daisy	12–24	various
Clarkia elegans	Clarkia	18–24	various
Collinsia	—	12–15	various
Convolvulus tricolor	Annual Convolvulus	12–18	various
Delphinium ajacis	Larkspur	24–36	pink, red, blue, white
Dianthus sinensis	Indian Pink	6–9	various
Eschscholzia	Californian Poppy	12	various
Gilia × hybrids	—	3–6	various
Godetia	Godetia	6–30	pink, crimson, white
Gypsophila elegans	Annual Gypsophila	18	white, pink, carmine
Helianthus annuus	Sunflower	36–96	yellow, bronze, brown
Helipterum	Everlasting	12	white, pink, yellow
Lathyrus odoratus	Sweet Pea	cl	various
Laverata trimestris	Mallow	24–36	white, pink
Leptosyne stillmanii	—	18	golden-yellow
Limnanthes douglasii	Butter and Eggs	6	white and yellow
Linaria maroccana	Annual Toadflax	9–15	various
Linum grandiflorum	Annual Flax	15–18	red, blue, pink, white
Lobularia	Sweet Alison	3–12	white, pink, lilac
Lupinus hartwegii	Annual Lupine	12–36	various
Malcolmia maritima	Virginia Stock	6–12	various
Malope grandiflorum	Mallow	24–36	pink, crimson, white
Matthiola bicornis	Night-scented Stock	12	lilac
Mentzelia lindleyi	Blazing Star	18	yellow
Nemophila menziesii	Baby Blue-eyes	tr	blue
Nigella damascena	Love-in-a-mist	18	blue, pink, white
Papaver rhoeas	Shirley Poppy	18–24	various
Papaver somniferum	Opium Poppy	18–36	various
Phacelia campanularia	—	9	blue
Reseda odorata	Mignonette	12–18	red, yellow, white
Rhodanthe manglesii	Everlasting	12	rose and white
Salvia horminum	—	18	blue
Saponaria vaccaria	Annual Soapwort	30	pink, white
Scabiosa atropurpurea	Sweet Scabious	18–36	various
Silene pendula	Annual Catchfly	6	various
Thelesperma burridgeanum	—	18	yellow, red-brown
Tropaeolum majus	Nasturtium	6 & tr	oranges, yellow, red
Tropaeolum peregrinum	Canary Creeper	cl	yellow
Viscaria oculata	Catchfly	6–12	various

Hardy Annuals to Sow in the Autumn

Botanical Name	Common Name	Height inches	Colour
Calendula officinalis	Pot Marigold	24	orange yellow
Centaurea cyanus	Cornflower	12–30	various
Cladanthus arabicus	—	30	yellow
Clarkia elegans	Clarkia	18–24	various
Delphinium ajacis	Larkspur	24–36	pink, red, blue, white
Eschscholzia	Californian Poppy	12	various
Godetia	Godetia	6–30	pink, crimson, white
Gypsophila elegans	Annual Gypsophila	18	white, pink, carmine
Iberis	Candytuft	6–15	various
Lathyrus odoratus	Sweet Pea	cl	various
Limnanthes douglasii	Butter and Eggs	6	white and yellow
Lobularia maritima	Sweet Alison	12	white, pink, lilac
Lychnis githago (syn. Agrostemma githago)	Corn-cockle	24–36	pale lilac
Malcolmia maritima	Virginia Stock	6–12	various
Nigella damascena	Love-in-a-mist	18	blue, pink, white
Oenthera biennis	Evening Primrose	30	yellow
Papaver rhoeas	Shirley Poppy	18–24	various
Saponaria vaccaria	Annual Soap-wort	30	pink, white
Scabiosa atropurpurea	Sweet Scabious	18–36	various
Specularia speculum-veneris	Venus's Looking Glass	9	blue
Viscaria	Catchfly	6–12	various

A Selection of Half-Hardy Annuals

Botanical Name	Common Name	Height inches	Colour
Ageratum	Ageratum, Floss Flower	6–18	blue
Amaranthus caudatus	Love-lies-bleeding	24	reddish-purple
Antirrhinum	Snapdragon	9–36	various
Arctotis hybrids	African Daisy	12–18	various
Begonia semperflorens	Begonia	6–9	white, pink, crimson

(continued from first column) Botanical Name	Common Name	Height inches	Colour
Brachycome iberidifolia	Swan River Daisy	15	white, pink, blue
Callistephus	Annual or China Aster	9–30	various
Celosia cristata	Cockscomb	12–18	yellow, scarlet
*Cobaea scandens	Cups and Saucers	cl	purple and green
Cosmos bipinnatus	—	36–48	various
Cosmos sulphureus	—	18	orange
Dimorphotheca aurantiaca	Cape Marigold, Star of the Veldt	12–18	orange, buff, salmon, white
Eccremocarpus scaber	Chilean Glory Flower	cl	orange-scarlet
Ipomoea purpurea	Morning Glory	cl	various
Kochia scoparia trichophila	Summer Cypress	12–36	foliage scarlet in autumn
Limonium bonduellii	Annual Statice	12–18	yellow
Limonium suworowii	Annual Statice	18–24	bright rose-pink
Lobelia erinus	Lobelia	6	blue, red, white
Matthiola incana	Ten-week Stock	12–15	various
Mesembryanthemum criniflorum	Livingstone Daisy	tr	various
Mimulus tigrinus	Annual Musk	12	various
Nemesia strumosa	—	9–12	various
Nicotiana	Flowering Tobacco	15–36	white, reds
Petunia	Petunia	9–18	various
Phlox drummondii	Annual Phlox	9–12	various
Portulaca grandiflora	Sun Plant	3	various
Rudbeckia Tetra Gloriosa	Gloriosa Daisy	36	various
Salpiglossis sinuata	Salpiglossis	12–30	various
Salvia splendens	Scarlet Salvia	9–15	scarlet
Tagetes	French and African Marigolds	6–36	various
Ursinia	—	9–18	various
Venidio-arctotis	—	18–24	various
Venidium fastuosum	—	30	various
Verbena hybrids	—	12	various
Zinnia	Zinnia	9–30	various

Annuals for Cutting

Botanical Name	Common Name	Height inches	Colour
Amaranthus caudatus	Love-lies-bleeding	24	reddish-purple
Arctotis hybrids	African Daisy	12–18	various
Calendula officinalis	Pot Marigold	24	orange yellow
Callistephus	Annual or China Aster	9–30	various
Centaurea cyanus	Cornflower	12–30	various
Chrysanthemum carinatum	Tricoloured Chrysanthemum	24	various
Chrysanthemum coronarium	Crown Daisy	12–24	various
Clarkia elegans	Clarkia	18–24	various
Cosmos bipinnatus	Cosmos	36–48	various
Cosmos sulphureus	Cosmos	18	orange
Delphinium ajacis	Larkspur	24–36	various
Dimorphotheca	Cape Marigold	12–18	orange, salmon
Gypsophila elegans	Annual Gypsophila	18	white, pink, carmine
Helichrysum bracteatum	Everlasting	24	various
Lathyrus odoratus	Sweet Pea	cl	various
Matthiola	Stocks	12–15	various
Limonium	Annual Statice	12–14	various
Moluccella laevis	Bells of Ireland	18–30	green and white
Nigella damascena	Love-in-a-mist	18	blue
Phlox drummondii	Annual Phlox	9–12	various
Scabiosa atropurpurea	Pincushion Flower, Sweet Scabious	18–36	various
Tagetes	African and French Marigolds	6–36	various
Tropaeolum majus	Nasturtium	6 & tr	oranges, yellow, red
Zinnia elegans	Zinnia	9–30	various

A Selection of Annuals for the Greenhouse

Botanical Name	Common Name	Height inches	Colour
Ageratum	Ageratum, Floss Flower	6–18	blue
Alonsoa	Mask Flower	12–24	scarlet, pink
Calendula officinalis	Pot Marigold	24	orange, yellow
Celosia cristata	Cockscomb	12–18	yellow, scarlet
Clarkia elegans	Clarkia	18–24	various
Exacum affine	—	12–15	violet, blue
Felicia bergeriana	Kingfisher Daisy	6–9	blue and yellow
Impatiens balsamina	Balsam	24	rose, scarlet, white
Ipomoea purpurea	Morning Glory	cl	various
Mimulus tigrinus	Annual Musk	12	various
Nemesia strumosa	Nemesia	9–12	various
Nicotiana affinis	Flowering Tobacco	15–36	white, reds
Primula malacoides	—	12–18	mauves, pinks
Salpiglossis sinuata	Salpiglossis	12–30	various
Schizanthus	Poor Man's Orchid, Butterfly Flower	12–24	various
Senecio cineraria	Cineraria	18–24	various

cl=climbing   tr=trailing.   *= perennials usually treated as annuals

EVERLASTING FLOWERS

1

The natural everlasting flowers are those with papery petals, often called immortelles, that can be dried and kept for indoor arrangements during the winter. The most common are helichrysums and other members of the daisy family including helipterum, ammobium, anaphalis and xeranthemum, all yellow, bronze, gold, pink and white and a packet of seeds can produce a lovely selection. The sea lavenders, too, are popular. They are often called statice, but belong to the genus *Limonium*, and they include the two annuals, *L. sinuatum*, in various colours and *L. suworowii*, bright rose, and the perennial *L. latifolium*, with tiny blue flowers. If they are kept free from dust they will last for years. The latter is sometimes dyed because the blue flowers tend to lose their colour and the gold, red and bright green flowers sold by florists in Christmas decorations were originally blue.

Cultivation and harvesting All these plants revel in a hot dry summer and last much better after a good season. Sow them in the greenhouse in March to get an early start, planting them out in May. Or sow in the open ground in the sunniest spot in the garden in late April and May, thinning the seedlings to 6 inches apart, and hope for a dry summer. Be prepared to sacrifice garden decoration for winter display because these flowers for drying need to be cut just as they come to maturity. If they are left two or three days too long the petals are less closely folded over one another and they soon shatter once they are completely dry. Cut them all with stems as long as possible, except perhaps the helichrysums, which often have lateral flower buds. These can be snipped off just behind the head and later given false stems. Tie them loosely in small bunches and suspend them from a cord or wire stretched across a garage or spare room or spread them out on wire mesh frames where there is no dampness and no direct sun. The former will encourage rotting and the latter will bleach the colour away from the flowers. The stems of many flowers bend and are not strong enough to hold the heads. False stems can be made with florist's wire, straws, pipe cleaners or twigs.

Other plants which will dry There are other plants which will retain their colour and shape well after drying and which associate happily in arrangements with the true immortelles. *Achillea filipendulina* 'Gold Plate', and 'Coronation Gold', sea holly (*Eryngium*), thistles, teasels, the lanterns of *Physalis franchetii*, *Moluccella laevis*, (bells of

Ireland), echinops, ferns, grasses, gourds, montbretias, cornflowers, heathers, astrantias, lavenders, edelweiss and hops can all be preserved and used, provided they are cut just at the point of maturity and not left too long. Most of these can be dried in the same way as the true everlasting flowers, or laid on sheets of newspaper away from the sun, dampness or heat for a week or two until they are thoroughly dehydrated. Ferns benefit from pressing between sheets of paper under the carpet, or between sheets of blotting paper under a cool iron.

Drying leaves Leaves to accompany this material can be either copper beech, gathered just before they begin to dry, or green beech once it has assumed its golden autumn colour. Put the sprays of leaves into a tall container filled with a mixture of half water and half

2

3

1 A selection of everlasting Helichrysums provides many gaily-coloured flowers for winter use.
2 Moluccella laevis, Bells of Ireland, is a striking everlasting flower.
3 Limonium sinuatum is a useful annual to grow for dried flower arrangements.

glycerine, keep them out of direct sunlight until the leaves are silky and then press them under the carpet between sheets of newspaper.

Some leaves, especially the leathery ones such as holly, magnolia, rubber plant (*Ficus elastica*) and camellia, can be skeletonised by leaving them in a tub of rainwater until the outer parts of the leaves become slimy and can be rubbed away, leaving the framework of the leaf. This needs washing in clean water and drying on paper and can be encouraged to curl without breaking once it is quite dry.

All this material, together with the seed-heads of such plants as nigella, columbines, larkspurs, poppies, *Iris foetidissima*, (the gladdon iris) with its brilliant orange fruits, honesty (*Lunaria*) which needs to have the outer coats gently removed to reveal the silvery 'moons' between, the fluffy seed-heads of clematis, the cones of conifers, acorns, nuts and the old female catkins of the alder and other hedgerow or garden material, provides endless scope for dried arrangements for indoor decoration. Materials should be stored in boxes once they have been dried, until they are needed, otherwise they will gather dust and lose their fresh look.

True everlastings

True Everlastings or Immortelles are those flowers grown specifically to be dried. They are annuals and grow best in a sunny place.

Acroclinium roseum *syn. Helipterum roseum* is a well-known straw daisy with petals softer than those of its near relative *Helichrysum bracteatum*. It grows to about 2 feet tall and has daisy-like pink or white flowers of papery texture. In a good summer it should flower six weeks after it has been sown, so you can grow and dry it in the same year.

Ammobium alatum grandiflorum (everlasting sand flower) has silvery-white petals and a domed yellow centre. It does grow to 2 feet tall but its stems are short in proportion to its flower-heads and you may need to lengthen them when you come to arrange them.

Gomphrena globosa (globe aramanth or batchelor's buttons) was a favourite in Elizabethan gardens. It grows 12–18 inches high, has white, red or purple globular flowers and is half-hardy.

Perhaps the best known of all the everlastings is **Helichrysum bracteatum** (the straw flower) which include both 3–4 feet tall and shorter dwarf varieties. It has flowers rather like those of a stiff, shiny-petalled double daisy in an assortment of colours—orange, wine-red, apricot, yellow, gold and white.

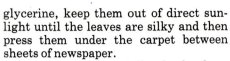

1 Anaphalis nubigena has silvery-white foliage and chaffy flowers.
2 The everlasting flowers of Ammobium alatum are silver and yellow.
3 Catananche caerula is a perennial everlasting for summer colour outdoors and winter decoration indoors.
4 Lonas annua is a South African Daisy with clustered papery flowers of yellow.
5 Dipsacus sylvestris, the native Common Teasel, grows up to 6 feet in height.

The flowers should be picked as soon as they begin to open.

Helipterum manglesii, also known as *Rhondanthe manglesii,* grows 12–18 inches tall and has tiny daisy flowers in clusters of florets—white, pink, or rose; both double and single blooms.

Statice (Limonium) sinuatum (sea lavender) grows 1–2 feet high and has papery flowers in blue, mauve, or white. Its perennial cousins are *Statice (Limonium) latifolium* which has mauve flowers—this is somewhat taller, reaching 2–3 feet—and *Limonium bonduellii* which has yellow flowers and grows to 1–2 feet. Both of these dry equally well.

Xeranthemum is another everlasting with silvery pink, mauve or white flowers. It grows to 2 feet tall and must be sown where it is to flower as it resents being moved.

Other flowers you can dry

There are also many perennials easily bought as plants or grown from seed which—although not true everlastings —have flowers, pods or seed heads which can be dried successfully. (Perennials are sown in summer for flowering the following year, or bought as plants and planted in spring or autumn.) With a little luck and a reasonable amount of care the most unexpected flowers can be dried—golden rod, cornflower, delphiniums, and double sunflowers.

Acanthus mollis (bear's breeches) with its tall spikes of white and purple flowers and large, jagged leaves grows to 3–4 feet and should be gathered when its lower florets are at their best. If you wait until these begin to fade the whole flower will fade and lose its colour.

Achillea is a yarrow which is found in many varieties from a few inches up to

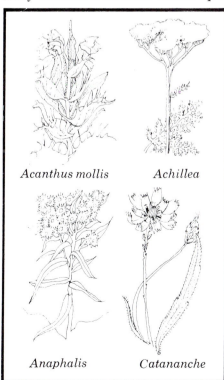

Acanthus mollis   *Achillea*

Anaphalis   *Catananche*

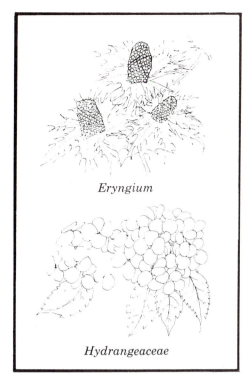

Eryngium

Hydrangeaceae

5 feet tall. It has flat white or yellow heads made up of a mass of tiny flowers and feathery grey-green leaves. This dries very well, and keeps its colour.

The silver-grey foliaged **Anaphalis** (pearl everlasting) has clusters of tiny everlasting-type daisy flowers and grows to 1–2 feet.

Catananche (blue cupidone or cupid's dart) has large blue daisy-like flowers and grows to 2–3 feet tall. It is one of the few which should be gathered when it is fully developed.

The prickly thistle family includes the superb silver-green and blue **Eryngiums** (sea holly) and the steely, blue metallic balls of **Echinops** (globe thistle). The thistle family as a whole provides a lot of interesting material in various sizes, all of which dry well and provide a bold contrast to the more fragile daisies.

Hydrangeaceae (hydrangea) is dried most successfully if it is arranged in fresh water and then just forgotten and left. Pick it when it is just changing colour, from blue to green and pink to red. For some inexplicable reason one or two blooms usually fail to dry well— remove these and keep the rest.

Grasses

Ornamental grasses are annuals and absolutely gorgeous for dried decorations. They flower in late summer and are sown and dried in the same way as flowers. (But the darker the place you dry them in the better; given a little light they turn pale and brittle.) Many of these set seed easily so grow them by themselves—they can be a nuisance in a mixed border.

Most reputable seedsmen sell good selections of grasses and below are listed just a few of those growable from seed. There are many more, some perennial,

from the common-or-garden wheat, barley, oats and millet right up to the giant 10 feet tall **Cortaderia argentea** (pampas grass) with its silvery plumes. They can be used on their own or mixed with dried flowers and look enchanting growing in rows or patches with their heads fluffy, furry, cloudy, wheat-like or woolly.

Agrostis nebulosa (cloud grass) grows to 1½ feet and has a charming head like a cloud of tiny flowers.

Briza maxima (pearl grass) and **Briza media** (quaking grass) have little hanging pendants or lanterns nodding in the breeze. They grow to 1–1½ feet and dry very well.

Coix lacryma-jobi (Job's tears) reaches 2–3 feet and has pea-sized seeds of pearly grey-green (which can be strung as beads) and thick leaves like maize.

Eragrostis elegans (love grass) has beautiful panicles (loose irregular arrangement of flowerheads) of cloudy florets, and grows to 2–3 feet.

Festuca ovina glauca (sheep's fescue) is a blue tufted grass with pretty small spikes of flower. This is one of the shorter grasses, rarely exceeding a height of 6 inches.

Hordeum jubatum (squirreltail grass) grows up to 2 feet and has feathery silver-grey flower heads on spiky wiry stems. Cut this young or the tails will disintegrate.

Lagurus ovatus (hare's tail) with its strong stems and fluffy, silky soft heads can be used fresh or dry.

Triticum spelta (ornamental wheat) is very decorative with a name that speaks for itself.

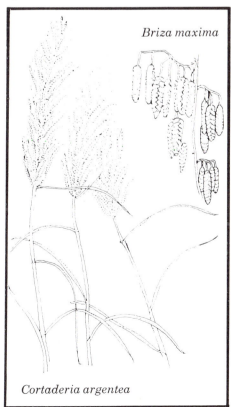

Briza maxima

Cortaderia argentea

CUT FLOWERS

One of the greatest joys of a garden is that with a little planning the gardener can have plenty of flowers and foliage for indoor decoration at all times of the year.

Even when done carefully, repeated cutting from the borders robs the garden of much of its decorative value. It is wise to grow plants just for cutting and any odd corner of the garden can be used for this but the best plan is to grow them in rows in the vegetable garden where they will get plenty of light, and the hoe can be worked around them when the vegetables are hoed. Annuals, perennials, ornamental gourds, grasses and even wild plants can be grown to provide material.

How to grow suitable material. Sow annuals in April or May in rows 9 inches apart and thin them to 6–8 inches apart according to the size of the ultimate plant. The thinnings can always be transplanted, either to some

other part of the garden or to make another row for cutting. The hardy annuals, such as asters and sweet peas, and perennials treated as annuals, such as antirrhinums, which need special treatment, should not be forgotten.

Biennials are grown from seed sown in rows in May and thinned in the same way as annuals, but later in the year the plants are best if they are transplanted. This makes them stockier plants, less likely to run to early flower, although the flower arranger might enjoy having Siberian wallflowers or honesty in September.

Plant perennials 2–3 feet apart to allow the plants to develop well and divide the clumps when they get either too congested or bare in the middle. In general they benefit from a spring mulch of compost.

What to grow Try to vary the annuals, biennials and vegetable material and plants for drying each year so that there can be a constant change of design in flower arrangement from year to year as well as from season to season. Seedmen's catalogues provide many ideas and recommendations and usually indicate the new strains of annual flowers which are always worth trying for a colour break or better constitution.

If some perennials fail, try others better suited to the position or if pyrethrums, especially the double varieties, give disappointing results, change to another variety because some of them seem to be very fussy about their surroundings.

Foliage is probably more important than anything else, and plants with leaves of interesting shape, texture or colour need to be included. Quite often these can be taken from the hedgerows, greenhouse or the rest of the garden, but consider planting in the cutting border some of the hostas for the value of their ribbed and undulating leaves, grey and silver-leaved plants, for example the senecios and artemisias, the purple-leaved *Phormium tenax purpureum* and the spotted pulmonaria or *Polygonum cuspidatum variegatum*. Grasses, some of them annuals, are always useful and do not overlook those plants that dry well and provide material for winter use. Several plants can be used after pressing under the carpet in sheets of newspaper or blotting

Many kinds of flowers are grown specifically for cutting.
1 'Serenade' is one of the Russell Lupins, useful for unusual and sophisticated flower arrangements.
2 Border pinks are useful for less formal cottage arrangements.
3 Erigeron 'Merstham Glory' is a semi-double flower for cutting in summer.
4 Papaver orientale, the Oriental Poppy, of which there are several varieties, both single and double, flowers for cutting in late spring and early summer.

paper. The flattened flower spikes of *montbretia* and many ferns can be preserved in this way.

Cutting It is the treatment the plant material receives at the time of cutting that determines whether it is going to last as long as possible or not in water. Naturally, some flowers do not last well whatever treatment is given and almost no material lasts quite as long once it has been cut as it would if left on the plant.

Always make a good clean cut when taking material from the plant, using scissors, secateurs or a sharp knife. In a very few instances, for example bergenia and heuchera, the stems should be pulled from the plant. There are special flower cutting scissors which have double blades, the one cutting the stem and the other gripping it at the base. These are extremely useful when one hand is holding aside other plants, for with the one hand the stem can be cut from the plant and carried back to the box or basket in which material is being collected without the bloom falling and getting bruised.

If the weather is particularly warm, it is worth taking a bucket of water to the plants and plunging the stems into this as soon as they are cut. This is essential for plants such as bergamot and calthas. Hollow-stemmed plants such as delphiniums should have their stems blocked by the thumb the moment they are cut and the hand not removed until it is below the water in the bucket. Further, delphinium spikes once cut can be turned upside down and the stems filled with water from a jug, plugged with cotton wool and then put into the bucket of water.

When to cut A general rule is not to cut material during the heat of the day but to collect it in the early morning or evening. Evening is perhaps the better time, when the flowers can be given a long drink in a cool place overnight and arranged the following day. Some material such as *Achillea millefolium* will flag when cut during the warm part of the day.

Most flowers need to be cut in bud if they are to last. This applies particularly to tulips, daffodils, paeonies, poppies, iris, roses, and most annuals. Kniphofias (red hot pokers), lupins and antirrhinums need cutting before the flowers at the bottom of the spike begin to fade. They will then curl a little in water and continue to be attractive until all the flowers are open, frequently dropping the older flowers; but the flower dropping is considerably reduced if the spikes are taken from the plant early enough.

The range of flowering plants that last well when cut is large and varied.
1 Delphiniums
2 Herbaceous paeonies
3 Crocosmis masonorum

Nicotiana 'Lime Green'

Salvia horminum 'Blue Bird'